From

"The Teacher Down the Hall"
Seminar Series

*All behaviors are choices;
All behaviors are learned;
All behaviors can change.
Choose Wisely!*

For every parent, teen, and teacher
who has ever asked the question:

"What did you do THAT for?"

*Peace,
Tod*

A Lesson Plan
for understanding what lies
behind every behavior.

By
Tod Faller

Graphics by Brian Faller

"What did you do THAT for!"

By

Tod Faller

copyright ©2005 Tod Faller

All rights reserved. No part of this publication may be reproduced or transmitted in any other form or for any means, electronic or mechanical, including photocopy, recording or any information storage system, without written permission from Headline Books, Inc.

To order additional copies of this book or for book publishing information, or to contact the author:

Headline Books, Inc.
P.O. Box 52
Terra Alta, WV 26764
www.headlinebooks.com

Tel/Fax: 800-570-5951 or 304-789-3001
Email: tod@todfaller.com
www.todfaller.com

ISBN 092991533X

Library of Congress Control Number: 2004112227

PRINTED IN THE UNITED STATES OF AMERICA

DEDICATION

To those who continue to inspire me:

The marvelous staff, students, and community of Ashton Elementary School.

Those who have dedicated careers to the service of children, as professional educators and service professionals.

The lady that is still my best friend after 35 years of marriage, my wife Irene... and an award winning teacher and elementary school principal.

My Graphic Designer son Brian, my business partner, lifelong friend, and creative resource.

My daughter-in-law Kerri, as one of thousands of dedicated Americans, for her courage and commitment to serve in our Armed Forces in hostile countries around the world.

Those who are open to understanding... who are willing to accept, rather than judge... who are willing to love, and to be loved.

My grandbabies.

And a special thank you to my friend, and fellow educator for 35 years, Diane Chandler. Before you retire from teaching and you and Frank ride off into the sunset on that Goldwing Motorcycle, thanks for proofing and offering your expertise on my last two manuscripts.

PREFACE

All humans want to be UNDERSTOOD and ACCEPTED. This is a fact of life. We want to understand WHY people behave the way they do. They frustrate us, they please us, they get in our way, and we can't understand why they don't always give us what we want. This is the source of our human conflicts.

To understand our CONFLICTS, and to answer the critical question, "What did you do THAT for?," the key is to understand both *how* and *why* we humans behave the way we do. It is in discovering how our differing perceptions, experiences, and human NEEDS so completely dictate our behaviors and impact our personal relationships. We dedicate far too much energy *reacting* to unwanted behaviors, and too little energy *responding* to the motivation behind the behavior. Conflict Resolution is all about learning to look past unwanted, inappropriate, or negative behaviors to resolve the CONFLICT that spawned those behaviors.

Because you live in a world with people in it, you already realize how our choices of BEHAVIORS can create conflicts, and separate us from our friends, family, customers, and clients. You know the anxiety and the discomfort this places upon your spirit, a spirit that would much prefer to live in peace, than conflict. You can now discover how an understanding of our common human BEHAVIORS and our human NEEDS can help bring us back together. YOU hold the power to RESOLVE conflict. When it comes to understanding and accepting human behavior, there is at least one constant — the more we are different, the more we are exactly alike. The gift we offer each other is NOT in UNDERSTANDING that we're different, but in ACCEPTING that we're different.

Everyone wants safer schools and places to work. Many of us are being asked to meet higher quotas, raise test scores, do more with less, and do it faster and better then we did last month or last year. The increased stress serves only to highlight our internal conflict and heighten tension with co-workers (faculty and staff) and clients (students and parents). Our unresolved *internal* conflicts become the *interpersonal* conflicts that sap our energy, divides relationships, separates teams, and robs us of our willingness to meet the increasing demands of work, home, and family.

While conflict can escalate into violence, this writing is NOT intended to address personality profiles, mental illness, or situations or relationships where unchecked conflicts have already escalated into physical threats or overt acts of violence. The premise of this text and "The Teacher Down the Hall" Seminar Series is conflict begins from within and *can* be resolved…but not until it is UNDERSTOOD and ACCEPTED.

Table of Contents

DEDICATION 3

PREFACE 4

Chapter 1
CONFLICT: It BEGINS from WITHIN 7

Chapter 2
You Want to Change the World?
Change Your Mind! 11

Chapter 3
The more we're DIFFERENT
The more we're EXACTLY alike 15

Chapter 4
Our Basic Human NEEDS 23

Chapter 5
Why DO we act that way? 39

Chapter 6
Controlling Behaviors:
When you won't take "NO" for an answer 57
The Stages of the Escalation of Control 66

Chapter 7
So, what do YOU want (NEED)? 69

"What did you do THAT for?"

Chapter 1

CONFLICT:
It BEGINS from WITHIN

Conflict is as natural as sunshine...and as prevalent as air.

"Philosophy doesn't rely on experiment or observation, only on one thing: THOUGHT."
—Thomas Nagel

Conflict is the uneasy feeling that you "forgot" something. It is that feeling that you may have embarrassed yourself at the party. It is wondering what to say to your teenager that won't upset him/her *this* time. It is the voice within that tells you how uncomfortable you are with the poor relationship that exists with your co-worker. It is the knot in your stomach that tightens every time you think about what you "should have" said after that argument you just had. Conflict is as natural as sunshine... and as prevalent as air. How to find a balance... how to COPE with CONFLICT... is what everyone wants to know.

"What did you do THAT for?"

> ...five basic human NEEDS: The NEEDS for
>
> 1.) Survival;
>
> 2.) Love and Acceptance;
>
> 3.) Affirmation and Fulfillment;
>
> 4.) Fun in our day
>
> 5.) The Freedom to make our own decisions.

Most professional approaches to resolve conflict are based on a century of accumulated knowledge and research on how the human brain works. Counselors use their considerable understanding to help us resolve the internal conflict and interpersonal conflicts in our lives. When we choose behaviors that keep us from maintaining emotional well-being, the counselor can help lead us back to awareness. Awareness can often come from just the understanding that our behaviors are nothing more than our best attempts at meeting our basic human NEEDS (Chapter 4). Our BEHAVIORS are the only way we have to act out our intentions and get us what we WANT (Chapter 5, 6). We will use behaviors throughout our lifetimes in never ending attempts to satisfy our NEEDS: The NEEDS for 1.) Survival; 2.) Love and Acceptance; 3.) Affirmation and Fulfillment; 4.) Fun in our day 5.) The Freedom to make our own decisions.

While there are many methods or approaches to counseling, all have the objective of helping people to meet their NEEDS. There are NO methods — NONE — that will work unless the person being counseled DECIDES to use it. This means that whether we seek professional counseling, have tea with a neighbor over the backyard fence, or choose to hold all of our fears, ambitions, doubts, and concerns inside ourselves, the only truly effective counseling is self-counseling.

Beyond seeing our high school counselor, most of us have never been to a professional counselor or even sought out literature to promote better mental health. Instead, we have become self-reliant on self-counseling. Sometimes we hear people say they don't need or want help because "There's nothing wrong with me." Others who have submitted to seeing a professional counselor may have done so as "a favor" to someone else "who really needed it." We wouldn't dream of being our own legal counsel, yet we won't seek the support of trained counselors when our emotional stability and peace of mind are at risk.

Meanwhile, still others among us know the relief that

comes with confiding in another human being. We realize it as a gift of life. We begin the shift from LIFE-draining to LIFE-giving, and say we feel a great weight lifted when we can "bare our souls." When we can think out loud, and place our ideas and fears in a safe and non-judgmental environment, we say it feels great "to get it off my chest." We know that our willingness to share and to open ourselves to others doesn't mean that we're weak or that we're "nuts." We are simply being permitted to test our thoughts against the patterns of thought that can be found in others.

Consequently, when we do so, we begin to understand and separate rational thought from irrational fears. These are fears that feed off of misperceptions, misunderstandings, and miscommunications. The more we read, understand, accept, open up to others, and *be open* to others, the more obvious it becomes: the more we're different, the more we're exactly alike (Chapter 3).

Carl Rogers, the father of Rogerian Counseling, believed that all the answers to life's questions are already within us. We can, he insisted, resolve our own internal conflicts. Sometimes we just need some guidance, someone to help us "sort it all out." During these times of internal conflict, Rogers likened that feeling to being trapped in a well.

Imagine being in the bottom of a deep, dark, cold well. You scream and cry for help, but there is no one to hear you. The longer you remain in that well, the more your fears deepen as loneliness and despair grip you like a vise. The absolute isolation becomes harder and harder to accept. Your mind wanders, your thoughts become distorted, your stomach is in knots, your head and body ache, and your screams, for all practical purposes, might as well be shouted in complete silence.

Then, suddenly, you hear a voice. Your cries for help have been heard. From the top of the well comes the invitation you have been waiting so long to receive: "I'm here to help you." Someone is offering you a lifeline. In that moment, you experience an explosion of joy within you as you realize that your safety, your happiness, your life itself is being handed to you by this person.

> Imagine being in the bottom of a deep, dark, cold well. You scream and cry for help, but there is no one to hear you.

> No one PUT you in this well, you jumped into it entirely on your own.

You want to know, "Who's out there?" Is it… a counselor, a friend, a family member, a co-worker, a stranger? Does it really matter? No one PUT you in this well, you jumped into it entirely on your own. Regardless of why you went in, you know now that you want out. You have your hand on the lifeline. Only YOU can DECIDE to begin the journey out. You need only to step beyond your pride to begin the climb. On the way you may find your answer to, **"What did you do THAT for?"**

Chapter 2

You Want to Change the World? Change Your Mind!

*The MIND is like a
parachute.
It does its best work when
it's open.*

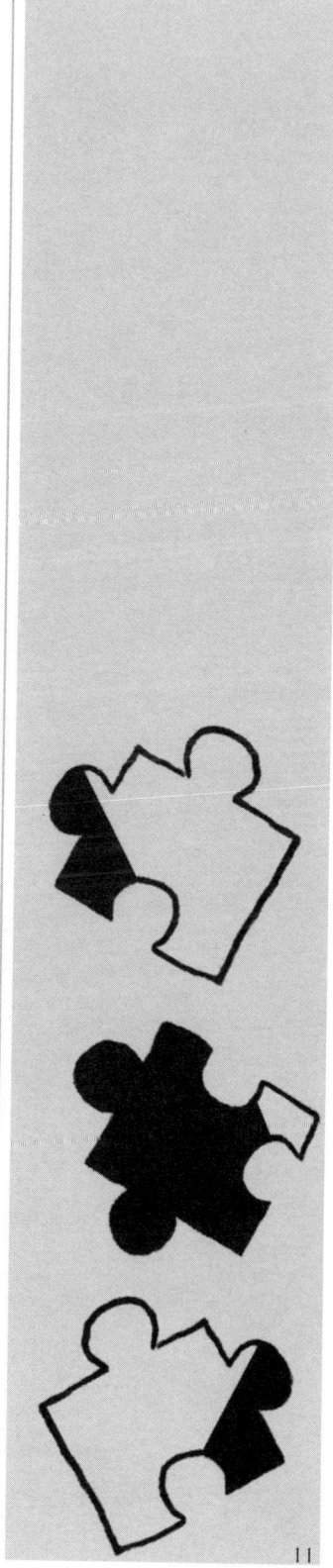

A little girl stood forlorn in her living room staring through the picture window out into the rain. Her father sat quietly in his chair reading his magazine, feeling sad that his young daughter could not go outside to play with her friends.

"I'll tell you what, honey," he said, "In this magazine I'm reading there is a picture of the world. What if I cut this picture into several pieces and make a puzzle for you? Would you like that?"

"Yes, Daddy," she said, and sat down on the floor by the side of the chair and began working on the puzzle her father had created for her. Meanwhile, father went back to his chair, content that the puzzle would keep her busy for quite some time. In just a few minutes, however, she stood up, smiled, and said, "Daddy, I'm finished."

"What did you do THAT for?"

> "We see the world the way we WANT it to be...NOT as it is."

Without looking, Dad smiled and said, "Honey, you can't be finished yet; there are a lot of pieces to the world."

"No, Daddy," she proclaimed, "You don't understand. On the other side was a picture of children. I just put the children together, and the world took care of itself."

Out of the mouths of babes! It doesn't matter what your status is, what you're being paid, your position on the staff, or what role you play in your family. If you work to bring "the children (people) together, the world will take care of itself."

Each one of us can intellectually accept that we can't change the world. We can't because each of us chooses our own attitudes, and we can't easily change our own attitudes, let alone the attitudes of others. If we want to change the world, we have to begin by changing our attitude. In order to change, we have to change our current understanding of why people act the way they do. The gift we offer each other is not just understanding that we are different, but accepting that we are different. To change the world, therefore, we must change the way we LOOK at the world.

Crudely stated, each of us believes that life is "ALL about Me." When asked to do something for another, there is a part of us that says, "What's in it for me?" We want to be first in line, we want to catch all the traffic lights green, we expect our lottery ticket to be THE lottery ticket, we want what we want when we want it, we get angry when others tell us no, we actually expect everyone to agree with us, and we see NOTHING wrong with this. Consequently, a great source of conflict stems from our inability NOT to see anything wrong with this. Like a child that stomps his foot to get his way, we insist on seeing the world the way we WANT it to be...NOT as it is. We persist in placing ourselves in conflict, rather than cooperation.

So what if we flipped the world over and looked at it from a completely different angle? Try to accept that everyone wants what you want... and everyone wants ONLY to meet their basic human NEEDS. And if

A Lesson Plan for understanding what lies behind every behavior.

everyone is trying to meet the SAME NEEDS as you are, what would happen if you worked to meet the needs of others... first?

This is what would happen!

If you work first to serve the NEEDS of others...OTHERS will go out of their way to meet YOUR NEEDS... Guaranteed! And the most astonishing fact is, they will do it willingly, and they won't even know why they're doing it. Maybe this sounds a bit too simplistic, but . . .

→ You CAN alter the behaviors of others.

→ You CAN change your attitude.

→ You CAN change the world... by changing the way you LOOK at your world.

And you can START RIGHT NOW.

READY?

What I'm going to be asking you to do first, is to PREPARE your MIND... to be OPEN to the possibilities. Prepare to ENTER every new encounter and RE-ENTER every relationship without expectation. I'm going to ask you to leave your judgments, preconceived notions, and heavy emotional baggage at the doorway to your mind. Wipe thoroughly, making certain that you leave BIAS and FEAR on the mat beneath your feet. With nothing to lose, and everything to gain, crack OPEN the door to your mind. Take the Risk. Shed any false pride that still clings to you. Take a deep breath... and prepare to step into faith. NO ONE can take this next step but YOU.

> Prepare to ENTER every new encounter and RE-ENTER every relationship without expectation.

"What did you do THAT for?"

Work to meet the NEEDS of others FIRST...

A kindergarten teacher once told a story about one of her students who was furiously at work drawing a picture. When the teacher saw her working, she asked the little girl what she was painting. Without hesitation, the little one said, "I'm painting the face of God."

Amused, the teacher said, "That's wonderful, honey, but no one has really ever seen the face of God to know what He looks like." As if shocked by the teacher's remarks, the child looked at her drawing...then looked back up at the teacher. Once again she looked earnestly at her drawing, then back up at the teacher. Finally, the little girl insisted, "They will when I'm finished!"

If you really want to change the world... take a risk... and be willing to change your mind. It CAN BE as easy as being OPEN to change... and to BEING changed. Try not to anticipate, and certainly, not to merely expect a change in OTHERS. A change in others will certainly occur, but that won't happen... it cannot happen... until you first realize a change in the MOST important person in your life... YOU. Work to meet the NEEDS of others FIRST... and the world will take care of itself. You may not be able to see it now, but like that little girl said to her teacher, "You will when I'm finished."

A Lesson Plan for understanding what lies behind every behavior.

Chapter 3

The more we're DIFFERENT... The more we're EXACTLY alike.

Communications is never in the intent of the speaker. Communications is always in the message received by the listener.

I have typed out four words or names in all CAPS below. I want you to cover all four words right now; find a note card, a book, a sheet of paper, or something. When I say GO, uncover and focus on just one word at a time. After looking at one name, close your eyes and just WAIT — three to five seconds; then go on, one at a time, through all four names. (You don't have to DO anything.) There are only four. READY...GO!

SUBWAY

KING KONG

HOWDY DOODY

CAPTAIN VIDEO
and the VIDEO RANGERS

"What did you do THAT for?"

> ...you instantly recalled some mental image you've attached to that experience.

You are living in the town you're in, working at the job you hold, partnering with the significant other you've chosen, and sitting at whatever station you are in life, as a direct result of the choices you have made to this point in your life. That is because we are are the sum total of our experiences. If we have lived it, it becomes a part of us. We base our future (decisions) on our past (experiences). The more experiences you have, the more input your "database" will receive to compute what you believe will be the best decisions for YOUR future. YOU are just so FULL of it (experience, that is)!

When you viewed each of those four words a moment ago, I didn't ask you to DO a thing. I didn't have to. Whether you wanted to or not, your experience or memory bank kicked in all by itself, and you SAW something. The tiny little photographer in your brain, the guy who takes snapshots of your experiences, also puts labels on these pictures so they can be identified for future reference and available for instant recall. We call those labels "WORDS."

As we recall experiences, we use WORDS to describe them. As we see or hear a word, we recall experiences that we associate with that word. The word, in this case, SUBWAY, is a label paper-clipped to a snapshot somewhere in your database that connects YOU, in some way, to an experience YOU have labeled "SUBWAY." You may have *seen* a picture of yourself eating a SUBWAY sandwich, you saw the SUBWAY sandwich sign while passing in a car, or you could have seen JARED doing a SUBWAY commercial.

You may have seen yourself sitting in a SUBWAY station, riding a SUBWAY, you read a book about SUBWAYS, or watched a movie that showed a SUBWAY. Perhaps just the prefix SUB brought up an entirely different picture. The point is, you SAW some memory reflective of "SUB" or "SUBWAY," whether you wanted to or not. If you EVER had an associated experience, in a flash, and without further external motivation, you instantly recalled some mental image you've attached to that experience.

A Lesson Plan for understanding what lies behind every behavior.

In the same manner, you then saw "KING KONG." Even in writing this, I remember seeing an early documentary as to how the original KING KONG movie was made. YOU saw something, too. It could have been anything from a story you heard (and visualized), to a clip from one of a dozen KING KONG movies, to seeing yourself eating a cupcake (that I just found out bears the same name). If you ever had an experience that your mind labeled KING (or) KONG, you SAW something.

When you read HOWDY DOODY, many of you went completely blank, didn't you? If you're an old feller like me, you saw Howdy the puppet "dancing" with Buffalo Bob or cracking jokes with Clara Bell the Clown. But if you NEVER had an experience (a mental picture) of something labeled "HOWDY DOODY," you could not possibly have pulled a memory from your hard drive that had NO information on "HOWDY DOODY."

I put CAPTAIN VIDEO and the VIDEO RANGERS in here, too, because many of you (if you'll admit it), knew who HOWDY DOODY was. Very few people, I'm sad to say, actually remember CAPTAIN VIDEO and the VIDEO RANGERS! He had a secret decoder ring that viewers could order so that they, too, could become a Video Ranger. When this television show first appeared (and soon disappeared), in the early 1950's, we pre-teens thought this spacemen show was pretty cool! (I can still SEE the OVALTINE commercials! Wow, now THERE is a blast from the past. But I digress…)

Just like the young folks who had no picture of Howdy Doody, if Captain Video was not part of YOUR experiences, try as you might, you drew a blank. Without an experience, the label (e.g. Captain Video) had NO significance. With NO picture (memory) of the event, there can be NO label. No Memory…NO Picture…NO word to describe it.

Now, let's take a minute to appreciate the significance of this discovery. The misunderstandings that come out of something as innocent as our failure to accept the gap that exists between one person's experiences (pictures of an event), and another is the "breeding ground" for CONFLICT. If you are a parent or a teacher, for

> If the child had no experience to attach to your words… the child would have NO frame of reference to understand you.

YOU TOLD THEM TO MAKE THEMSELVES AT HOME.

"What did you do THAT for?"

> ...did he (Dad) TEACH his child what he wanted, or did he just TELL his child what he hoped for?

example, think about the last instruction you gave a child. If the child had no experience to attach to your words—words coming out of YOUR world of experiences, the child would have NO frame of reference to understand you.

If you used words out of YOUR experience, and the feedback you received revealed nothing but a blank expression, NOW you know why. Either TEACH him a new word, or use words that you believe would better fit his limited world of experiences. It took you years to acquire your wealth of experiences. Young people just THINK they know what you do.

My wife, Irene, also a school principal, just looked over my shoulder and said, "Give them an example." Try this (not that I think you need it):

Remember when your mom said, "Don't touch the stove, it's HOT!" Sure enough, you had to test it for yourself. Was it because you couldn't trust your own mother? Or was it because you had no experience with which to compare? The last time mom said "hot," maybe she was referring to a "hot" sunny day. Your mind didn't, at that time, differentiate between "hot" and (a word you'd soon be learning...), SCALDING. Your previous experiences said "hot" is not so bad, so what's the big deal? But AFTER you touched the "hot" stove, the FEEDBACK you received (...and there will always be FEEDBACK), planted NEW pictures into your memory bank; pictures with labels like Pain, Fear, Trust Mother, and BAD Stove.

So as not to trivialize this example (and incur the wrath of the principal standing over my shoulder), let's do this one more time. When Dad said DO NOT ride your bike in the street, did he TEACH his child what he wanted, or did he just TELL his child what he hoped for? Did he teach his child, or just assume he would be understood? What is he to do with a child that has no experiences to compare? Dad, of course, may have once fallen off his bike, been scared by traffic, seen a movie about someone on a bike being hit by a car, or in any one of a few dozen ways EXPERIENCED, and now KNOWS, that this is dangerous. Dad learned by experience.

In Junior's absence of such experiences, will just telling him to keep his bike out of the street work? RIGHT! How many times have YOU said (or have YOUR parents said to YOU), "Don't make me tell you again!" Or "If I have to say this ONE MORE TIME..." The lesson here is obvious: You want it? TEACH IT!

Unless OTHERS have the SAME or very similar experiences as YOU do — ACCEPT it: others will NOT be able to KNOW what YOU KNOW. Therefore, you can't assume that OTHERS will understand your instructions merely because YOU do.

Communications is NEVER in the intent of the speaker, it is ALWAYS in the message received by the listener.

From purely an educator's perspective, if you remember nothing else from this, remember this cardinal rule for parents, teachers, principals, CEO's, or anyone:

"IF YOU WANT IT UNDERSTOOD,
don't say it, hope for it, or assume it... TEACH IT!"

AN ASIDE: When teachers or parents are explaining lessons and concepts, they can often slip into language out of their own world of understanding. It is my experience that most young people would rather FAIL, pretending to understand, then to admit in front of their peers, that they don't understand. Fearing a loss of acceptance, they seem to think that it makes them look "stupid" if they don't know even the meaning of a single word. Students seem blissfully unaware that if they don't know, then the vast majority of their classmates—all with similar levels of experience—probably won't know either. The truth is, the first student to raise his hand to ask the teacher for clarity would be viewed by the rest of the class (secretly, of course), as their hero.

Do you remember that expression, "The more we're different, the more we're exactly alike?" While MOST of us would agree that we are different from each other, what

> "IF YOU WANT IT UNDERSTOOD, don't say it, hope for it, or assume it... TEACH IT!"

"What did you do THAT for?"

> Our common quest to meet our NEEDS is the solitary reason why we choose all those behaviors in the first place.

we are really saying under our breath is, "YOU are different from ME."

It is as if each of us is saying, "I AM THE STANDARD" by which all humans are made, and anyone different from ME…is…well, obviously…WRONG! We then dedicate a lifetime in the attempt to get others to see the world as WE understand it…as we WANT it to be…as we think it SHOULD be.

It's a lot like marriage:
We spend half of our lives trying to find mates we're compatible with and the rest of our lives trying to change them!

We'll soon cover the process by which we choose our attitudes and perceptions and make expectations for ourselves based on the feedback we received from those experiences. Every experience YOU have ever had—the car rides, the sandbox, the walks along the ocean, the toys you played with, the God you prayed to, every book, magazine article or passage you've ever read, the friends you had, the people who loved you…or refused to love you…and even the last couple of minutes you've dedicated to the reading of this text—ALL go into the formation of YOU.

It is as if there was an invisible magic blender on your head. This blender serves to mix up every new experience you receive, blending and conflicting with all those other experiences, so that what comes out of you, with each new experience, makes you even MORE unique than you were just a few moments before. Every second is a new opportunity to make NEW choices! Your choices come out of YOUR world of understanding—and are RIGHT for YOU.

Now brace yourself, because EVERY OTHER individual on the planet is doing the SAME thing, every minute of the day, making himself or herself even MORE different, more unique…from YOU. EACH of us NEEDS to make creative, responsible decisions for ourselves. EACH one of us is DIFFERENT…we're just built that way.

A Lesson Plan for understanding what lies behind every behavior.

And YOU thought people who were different from you were just being obstinate, huh?

Psychologists say that each of us makes more than 50,000 decisions every single day. These decisions are what prompt our BEHAVIORS. The tens of thousands of behaviors EACH of us chooses every single day is what separates us and provides us with the perception that we humans are so vastly different. Yet, our inherent drive to satisfy just five basic human NEEDS is what we ALL have in COMMON. Our common quest to meet our NEEDS is the solitary reason why we choose all those behaviors in the first place. It is how we can accept that we are all exactly alike.

> ...each of us makes more than 50,000 decisions every single day.

- ✓ The gift we offer each other is not in UNDERSTANDING that we're different, but rather in ACCEPTING that we're different.

- ✓ Our BASIC HUMAN NEEDS are the reasons WHY we choose behaviors in the first place.

- ✓ Every behavior is an attempt to meet our NEEDS.

- ✓ First seek to meet the NEEDS of OTHERS, and OTHERS will begin tripping over themselves to meet YOUR NEEDS…and they won't even know why they're doing it!

  GUARANTEED!

"What did you do THAT for?"

Notes

"Take a minute to reflect. How are you different from those with whom you are in conflict?"

Chapter 4

Our Basic Human NEEDS

*"SERVICE isn't something to
DO, it's SOMEONE to BE."*
—Henry Noulin

There is a vast difference between what we NEED and what we WANT to survive and to mature as humans. The purpose behind everything you WANT is to meet at least one (1) of only five (5) basic human NEEDS. You can't always get everything you WANT, but you can always obtain some of what you NEED.

Take an example from my son Brian. While still a young adolescent, Brian sought to meet his NEED for LOVE and ACCEPTANCE. As he grew from childhood into adolescence and beyond, he naturally began to reach outside his family to keep reaching for this NEED. As a 14 year old, he chose behaviors that helped him meet this NEED by WANTING a girlfriend. Some of the BEHAVIORS he chose to meet this NEED were to take a bath, comb his hair, put on some of his brother's after shave...then beg her for a date. This was his best attempt, for his level of experience, to keep reaching for this (lifelong) NEED for unconditional LOVE and ACCEPTANCE.

> You can't always get everything you WANT, but you can always obtain some of what you NEED.

> If you work to SERVE these NEEDS in OTHERS – OTHERS will go out of their way to serve YOUR NEEDS... and they won't even know why they're doing it...

From the valentines for his "girlfriends" in grade school, to hand-holding on the playground, to a kiss on the cheek at the bus stop, his actions naturally escalated into never-ending attempt to meet this NEED for unconditional LOVE and ACCEPTANCE. As no single behavior will provide a quick fix or permanent solution to our NEEDS, Brian was able to find, with every attempt to be loved and accepted, that he was able to find some of the LOVE and ACCEPTANCE that he NEEDED, if not everything he WANTED.

As he grows into adulthood, thousands of behaviors (both at a conscious and at a subconscious level) will be spawned DAILY in attempts to meet this solitary NEED. In the same way, and at the same time, he'll also be choosing thousands of other behaviors in attempts to satisfy his other FOUR basic human NEEDS as well. And this pattern of choosing BEHAVIORS to satisfy these NEEDS will continue unabated until he dies.

The reason why these NEEDS are ESSENTIAL to understanding in a text that is trying to RESOLVE CONFLICT is this: If you work to SERVE these NEEDS in OTHERS—OTHERS will go out of their way to serve YOUR NEEDS… and they won't even know why they're doing it…GUARANTEED!

What follows are three different perspectives on these basic human NEEDS, from three highly respected psychologists/ psychoanalysts over the span of a century.

A Lesson Plan for understanding what lies behind every behavior.

Our HUMAN NEEDS: Perspective #1

C.G. JUNG:
The NEED to be AFFIRMED and ACCEPTED.

> Your body will not allow you to "deny the truth."

Carl Jung, a one-time student of Sigmund Freud, was a psychiatrist and psychologist who practiced through the early to mid-twentieth century. His works were numerous and his impact profound. Of his many contributions, his theory on human personality is still popular and used today as the premise for understanding personality profiles. His work emphasized that the "collective unconscious" was the source of ALL inspiration and instincts. With Freud, he referenced, "The *conscious* mind is like the water that rises from a fountain. The *unconscious* mind," he said, "is like a veritable ocean from which the fountain draws." Every experience is added to the ocean, ready to be recalled when beckoned by the conscious or unconscious mind. Body communications (or body language) can be understood with such an analogy.

Jung said that trying to hold back the unconscious mind, that is, trying to deny the truth, would be no different than trying to hold wood under water. One might be able to consciously suppress some thoughts or emotions, but the more one tries to hold them down, the harder it is to consciously keep covered whatever it is your unconscious mind is trying to bring to the surface. Your body will not allow you to "deny the truth." This is the premise behind our modern day polygraph, the lie detector.

Remember your first date? You told yourself (and your date) that you weren't nervous. Yet, you tripped over your tongue, spilled drinks, didn't know what to do with your hands, and your bumbling attempts to say goodnight on the doorstep all spoke loudly to the contrary. Just as you can't forever hold wood under water, you can't forever suppress the TRUTH that lies just beneath the surface. If you WERE nervous on that first date, as hard as you might have tried to suppress it, your body language cannot lie and will always reveal the truth.

"What did you do THAT for?"

> Every behavior is exercised for the express purpose of satisfying one of five basic human NEEDS.

Jung believed that the uniting of the conscious mind (the aware and "thinking" mind), with the unconscious mind, was the foundation from which humans found "wholeness and balance." As a lifetime scholar and practitioner, Jung was highly respected in his field. He dedicated his entire professional life to the study of the difference and similarities of man. In addressing our human NEEDS, Carl Jung offered these responses to what are known as, the two (2) "universal questions."

1. What motivates ALL people to act the way they do?

"ALL people NEED to be AFFIRMED: Each person NEEDS to be loved, praised, and respected."

2. What do ALL people have in common?

"ALL people have the NEED to be ACCEPTED, to be made to feel a part of a peer group. Consequently, people will act the way OTHER people want them to."

Our HUMAN NEEDS: Perspective #2

ABRAHAM MASLOW:
The NEED to be SAFE, LOVED and ACCEPTED, to achieve SELF-RESPECT and the RESPECT of others, and to be FULFILLED.

Abraham Maslow developed a theory in the late 1960's that identified our human NEEDS and illustrated how people could meet those NEEDS. Referred to as his Hierarchy of NEEDS, he believed that people naturally motivate themselves (to the exclusion of outside stimuli like awards, punishment, brownie points, and badges), to reach their own highest potential. He saw NEEDS as levels, in which all of our really basic NEEDS are at the bottom and must be achieved before climbing farther to reach our highest potential at the top. This is depicted in a pyramid. From the bottom to the top, the pyramid of NEEDS looks like this:

A Lesson Plan for understanding what lies behind every behavior.

5. **SURVIVAL** is at the bottom of the NEEDS pyramid. This is our NEED for food, water, and... survival!

4. **SAFETY** and **SECURITY**: Maslow believed that children are more fearful and more visually display fear and insecurity than adults. Nonetheless, valid fear and apprehension are also evident when this NEED is threatened or absent in adults.

3. **SOCIAL NEEDS**: This is our inward NEED to avoid loneliness and alienation. This is our NEED for affliations, to belong, to be loved, and to be accepted.

2. **SELF-RESPECT:** We strive (choose behaviors) to achieve self-respect, as well as the respect of our peers. This is our NEED to feel important and useful. The absence of self-worth can be debilitating. It can sap our strength and overpower us with a sense of inferiority or worthlessness.

1. **SELF ACTUALIZATION** or **FULFILLMENT** is at the top of the pyramid. Since no one can hope to stay at the top, we are constantly stretching to reach, grasp, and hold onto this level. People at this level, having reached fulfillment, are not content to just sit back and rest from the journey. These people have a mission! That is, they hold a vision, and work diligently and methodically to achieve great things. They seem to "fit" in the role they play, as one might see himself "called" to a career.

Self-actualized people like the view from the top!

> Self-actualized people like the view from the top! From there, the dreamer MUST seek out his dreams.

"What did you do THAT for?"

> You must look past the behavior to understand the NEED that spawned that behavior.

From there, the dreamer MUST seek out his dreams. Such people accept what they CAN do, and in turn, what they MUST do. If they do not, the endless restlessness, the knot in the stomach, or the relentless sense that "there is something else out there for me," will persist. The voice within will not rest until the dream is chased.

Our HUMAN NEEDS: Perspective #3

WILLIAM. GLASSER:
The NEED to be LOVED and ACCEPTED, POWERful or "IMPORTANT," to have FUN, and know FREEDOM.

Another popular view on our basic human NEEDS comes from Dr. William Glasser, founder of Reality Therapy (1965), Control Theory (1984), and Choice Theory (1998). Glasser's Choice Theory affirms that ALL of our behaviors are exercised for the express purpose of satisfying one of five basic human NEEDS. At any age, based on each person's unique experiences and perceptions, we are constantly choosing behaviors WE think will get us what we want. Although each of us is drastically different in our choice of behaviors, we are exactly alike in our inward desires to meet five basic NEEDS.

1. **SURVIVAL**: As Maslow indicated, this is the most basic of our human NEEDS. It requires such essentials as food, shelter, and even the basic sexual drive to prevent extinction of the species.

2. **LOVE** and **BELONGING**: As with Jung and Maslow, Glasser, too, believed that ALL of us NEED to be unconditionally LOVED, to be genuinely ACCEPTED, taken seriously, and be truly understood. It is not a birthright afforded some; it is inherent in ALL humans that we be treated with dignity, equality, and respect.

3. **POWER**: This is NOT saying that we need to be IN POWER, to hold power, or to be in positions of power or authority. Instead, as Jung phrased it, think of it as having the NEED to be AFFIRMED: to be fulfilled, positively recognized, really listened to, and acknowledged with a sense of value or importance. Maslow might recognize this as being similar to his description of our human NEED for SELF-RESPECT.

4. **FUN**: Regardless of our unique gifts and talents, different personality types, and varying styles of learning, Glasser alone says we have a common NEED for FUN in our lives. FUN can best be recognized in the explosion of joy we know as laughter. It fills the heart and opens the mind to a new willingness to learn. Organizations actually have a name for the level of FUN within their ranks; they call it morale.

5. **FREEDOM**: Each of us seeks to be INDEPENDENT, to make creative and responsible decisions for ourselves. To deny the freedom of another assumes superiority, perpetuates dependence, enables, and withholds from others the very same freedoms we seek for ourselves.

Hopefully, you are now growing more confident in your understanding of our human NEEDS. For in this understanding lies the certainty that behavior is merely each person's best attempt at getting his or her NEEDS met. You do NOT have to choose to take personally the behaviors that others choose. It is NOT about YOU. It IS about others seeking a behavior(s) to meet *their* NEEDS. Know that others don't necessarily intend to hurt or offend you with their choices of behaviors. They are merely choosing behavior(s) *their* experiences have taught them would offer the best chance(s) of getting them

> You do NOT have to take the behaviors of others personally...

> Remember, (the behavior of others), it is **not** about you.

what they wanted... THIS time... to get them some of what they NEED. Everyone has the right to meet their NEEDS as long as they do not infringe upon the rights of others in meeting their own needs.

While all of us are capable of displaying an endless array of behaviors, remember that EACH behavior serves only to satisfy one or more of these basic human NEEDS. You couldn't possibly be expected to know or understand every BEHAVIOR that is directed towards you. However, you CAN, most DEFINITELY, learn to look past the behavior to see the NEED that person is trying to meet. Understanding these five basic human NEEDS is the foundation for CONFLICT RESOLUTION.

Take a minute now to "Check for Understanding."

Remember that to answer the question, **"What did you do THAT for?"** you must be willing to look beyond the BEHAVIOR. You must look past the behavior your getting, to understand the NEED that spawned that behavior. It is easier to do if you truly understand that the behavior is intended to meet *their* need—and is truly **not** about you!

Ok, now imagine what would happen if TODAY you ACTUALLY started to look PAST the negative behaviors of the person that is being such a pain in your... life.

READY?

FIRST, think of a person in your life with whom you are experiencing CONFLICT. You will know who this person is immediately because in just thinking about him (her), your stomach will begin to tighten. A moment later, that face will flash before your eyes. Got it? Try the following exercise:

By looking at the NEEDS that follow, ask yourself these two questions:
1. "What specific behavior(s) is this person displaying that troubles me so much?" and,

A Lesson Plan for understanding what lies behind every behavior.

2. "What NEED could this person possibly be hoping to satisfy by acting out this particular BEHAVIOR?"

Follow these three steps to get your answer:

1. First separate yourself from the emotion… the pain, hurt, disappointment…whatever. (Remember, it's NOT about you.)

2. Isolate or identify the negative or non-productive BEHAVIOR(s) being displayed.

3. NOW…look beyond the BEHAVIOR to understand the NEED he (she) is trying to meet. (What does he really WANT? What is he trying so hard to tell me with this behavior?) It will be one of these five (5) NEEDS:

➤ Is he (she) trying to meet his **SURVIVAL** NEED… for food, clothing and shelter?

➤ Does he NEED to be **LOVED** and ACCEPTED…by me…or his peers?

➤ Does he NEED to be **AFFIRMED** or FULFILLED…recognized as important, valued, or really listened to?

➤ Does he NEED to have some **FUN** in his day?

➤ Does he NEED to have the **FREEDOM**… to make creative, responsible, and independent choices for himself?

NOW…really focus on this…what NEED do you think is driving that behavior(s)?

GOT YOUR ANSWER?

…pride is a formidable obstacle to hurdle…

"What did you do THAT for?"

Can you determine what NEED is behind your teenager's controlling BEHAVIORS?

Once you believe you understand the NEED behind the BEHAVIOR, this is why you want to know.

Remember that people will always want things they can not have. That is, people CAN'T always have everything they WANT. Remembering, too, that people can ALWAYS have some of what they NEED, you are now in a position NOT to take their behavior personally and to help them get some of what they NEED.

This person you selected is using behaviors to get what he (she) WANTS...but YOU now know what he really NEEDS...what he NEEDS and is trying to satisfy through YOU. This is tough—as pride is a formidable obstacle to hurdle—but if you can look past the hurt from those nasty or inappropriate behaviors and begin to SERVE the missing NEED he/she is trying to meet, you will know almost instantly if you are right. He will begin treating YOU differently...more positively...and HE won't even know why he's doing it...GUARANTEED!

STOP...before going on...

Realize that I did not say, "give him (her) what he WANTS." I said, you can give him some of what he NEEDS. People only choose BEHAVIORS to meet their NEEDS. This fact is so critical to understanding how to resolve conflicts with your teens, spouse, teachers, parents, and co-workers, that I'm going to ask you to go though this exercise again.

Pick a different person and a different behavior.
Got him (her)?
Got that behavior in mind?
Now, what NEED is this person trying to satisfy?

With just the simple acceptance that ALL OF US will choose BEHAVIORS to meet our NEEDS, this should be of great comfort to you. That is, YOU do NOT have to take negative displays of behaviors personally... because it's NOT about you.

A Lesson Plan for understanding what lies behind every behavior.

It IS about someone ELSE trying to meet HIS (or her) NEEDS…and trying to go through YOU to make it happen. Try to think of it this way. Although it may be processed at an unconscious level, he is simply trying to get one (or more) of his NEEDS met, and is seeking YOU out to get YOUR help. (Makes you feel kind of proud, doesn't it?)

Let's go through this exercise just once more. This time, imagine that we're talking about your daughter (or son).

PROBLEM: Can you determine what NEED is behind your teenage daughter's controlling BEHAVIORS to get YOU to release the car keys so she can "go for a spin with her friends?" Why do you think your junior miss is trying to make you feel guilty for not buying those $100 school shoes you can't afford? And why do you imagine that she would pout and choose to scream, "I hate you!" because you wouldn't allow her to stay out until 2:00 in the morning?

Remember, there is NO need to take it personally. These are just her best attempts, from her limited experiences and understanding, to meet her NEEDS. Remind yourself... this is NOT about you.

STEP ONE: Answer this important question: "What NEED is she trying to satisfy with these Behaviors?" Take a minute to think about it. (Look at her BEHAVIORS again...and then that list of NEEDS— see page 31.)

If you were able to look past these behaviors (instead of being shocked, angry, or disappointed), you were probably able to identify the NEED that was behind her actions. In this case, you probably realized that she was trying to meet her NEED for ACCEPTANCE from her peers, what Glasser calls Love and Belonging. It takes a little practice, but come on, there are only four NEEDS to consider. (Yes, there are really five NEEDS, but I'm sure you realize that we're not talking about her SURVIVAL NEED here.)

> Through the seventh and eighth grades, a stranger takes over the body of the child you used to call son or daughter.

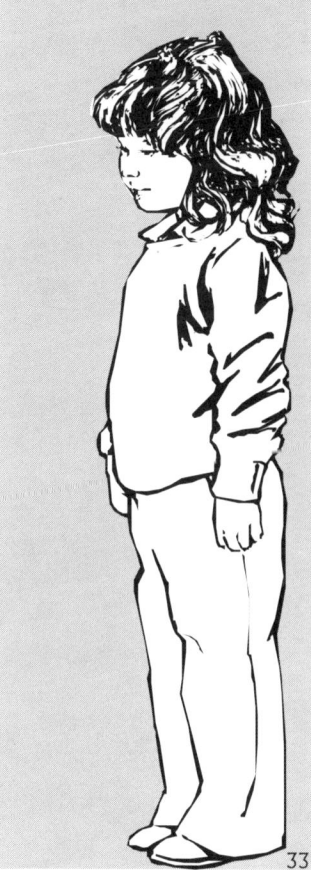

"What did you do THAT for?"

> To a teenager, EVERYTHING depends on the answers to these two questions.

STEP TWO: Answer this all-important question: "Now that I've established what NEED was driving her Behaviors, how can I help her get some of what she NEEDS, even if she can't have everything she WANTS?" Your answer to that question can go a long way toward cementing your relationship. It will also go a long way toward resolving existing conflict and diminishing the prospects of conflict rearing its ugly head in the future.

AN ASIDE: Young people, particularly teenagers, are not complex, so they are fairly easy to read. You begin to really notice the changes around the fifth or sixth grade when the hormones kick in and the child you reared begins to transform. Through the seventh and eighth grades, a stranger takes over the body of the child you used to call son or daughter. As they progress through their teen years, the goofy period passes and takes on a more sophisticated air. But the same two questions that have dominated their lives since middle school still need answered. Their behaviors are dictated by their peer's response to these two critical questions. To a teenager, EVERYTHING depends on the answers to these two questions.

1. "How good do I look?"

2. "How many friends do I have?"

This is an oversimplification, of course (not by much…), but if you are a teacher or a parent, it might help in better understanding your teenager(s). As a teenager moves through life, all behaviors keep pointing back to these same concerns. I believe that the level of your teenager's "Self Esteem," the extent to which he (or she) will choose happiness or choose misery in his (or her) life, will be in direct proportion to the degree of acceptance he finds behind each question — the answer he hopes to find behind each behavior.

"Yes, I am STILL ACCEPTED by my peers!"

In "real life," as with the examples in this exercise, you're looking for a WIN-WIN response… when

A Lesson Plan for understanding what lies behind every behavior.

possible. What CAN you do when your inexperienced sixteen-year-old daughter wants the keys to the car to go for "a spin?" When you were sixteen, surely you remember that it was "way cool" to have your driver's license, but it did little good if you had no one to impress with it. I mean, it's great to show it off at school, but until "THEY" see you driving around with it...so what? Yeah, it's coming back to you now, isn't it? (...saw a few flashback memories, huh?)

For "your daughter's" sake, you feel badly, maybe even a little guilty, because you know she just wants to fit in, to be accepted, to impress "the gang." But your inner voice is telling you "WHOA, hold on, Child!" You want to protect her — you want her to be safe — you're torn between her NEED for Acceptance and your own NEED for Acceptance by protecting someone you love. How can you let her go? You know you don't want to say, "OK, Dear, have a great time," then pace the floor until she returns.

And you SURELY don't want to say what you're thinking — "NO WAY!"— because then you'll have to deal with the conflict that will certainly follow the mock indignation and the "you don't trust me," and the "you're ruining my life" lines.

So what CAN you do to eliminate or at least diminish this conflict?

Start with that critical question: "How can I help her to meet her NEEDS (peer ACCEPTANCE), without giving her a blanket (all that she WANTS), "OK, here are the keys,... see ya later." You start by realizing that she already has enough friends. She is COUNTING on YOU to be her parent. She needs YOU to teach her responsibility and to provide the STRUCTURE or boundaries in her life. So provide it! Instead of conflict, offer her some "Responsibility Training."

You can agree, for example, to the "spin" in the car, but you get to define the trip for her. Consider specifying the duration of the trip, or the mileage the trip can cover.

> She already has enough friends. She is counting on YOU to be her parent...

> Yes, her "I hate you!" words can sting, but your experiences (memories) of her loving you are always ready for immediate recall.

Perhaps she can deliver something for you to her uncle's house (to check in). Does she get to go in the daylight or dark? YOU can limit the riders. Maybe you'll want to select her co-pilot. You might ask her to take this "spin" on an errand for you to a nearby shop or pizza pick-up. She can stop at the gas station and (with her money?) fill up the car. (And she did make her portion of the insurance payment to show some ownership for the responsibility of driving, right?)

Based on your own circumstance, I'm sure you're already thinking of other ideas as well. The point is, you are offering her SOME of what she NEEDS, if not everything she WANTS.

In the same manner, how can you offer her SOME of what she NEEDS (still looking for peer acceptance), when she insists on those $100 shoes (or designer pants, the name brand tops, the fancy bracelet…)?

And what's up with this staying out until two in the morning? You know that ultimately, regardless of her behaviors to control or guilt you, there is no way you're going to fold on her staying out until 2 a.m. — right? The operative word in allowing your daughter, in allowing anyone, to make "creative, responsible decisions for herself" is *responsible*. Is this a responsible request from a 16 year old? Would permitting her to do this be a responsible decision on your part... the responsible adult?

You also know that she DOES love you, regardless of her obvious attempt to control you with that snappy, "I hate you!" comeback. When you looked past that behavior, you saw through it, didn't you? You KNOW she meant just the opposite, because she tells you she loves you every day — without saying a word.

Yes, her "I hate you!" words can sting, but your experiences (memories) of her loving you are always ready for immediate recall. You know you're loved when your experiences remind you that YOU were the one she wanted to tuck her into bed every night. She wanted your hug after saying her nightly prayers. After her first broken heart it was your comforting voice and touch she wanted.

And you are the one she still clings to when she is hurt, sad, or lonely and wants consoled. You are the one she runs to when she is at her best, happy, and at the top of her game. And you are the one she asks to help her with a puzzle, to play cards or a board game, to go shopping with, to share secrets, to answer those boy questions, to help her with homework, to listen to her, and so on and so on.

And you know for sure she has always loved you each time she offered you that award-winning smile when she WASN'T imagining that you were "ruining her life" by not allowing her to "hang out" until two in the morning. Her need for peer ACCEPTANCE is strong, but her NEED for YOUR LOVE is SO powerful that if you don't provide it, she will act out (DEMANDING IT) until you do. While it is true that you want to be positive and say "YES" as often as possible, understand, too, that "NO" is an acceptable answer. It is also what she occasionally needs just to be reassured that her boundaries are still in place.

Give your kids some credit. I'm sure it has already occurred to you that this young lady, like most teens, might REALLY WANT you to say "NO." Her NEED is to be accepted by her peers (she already has YOUR acceptance), so it is much easier to say "NO" to you, and "YES" to her friends. What if she could go back to her friends and say, "I WANTED to go with you (out until 2 a.m., to buy those $100 shoes, to go for a "spin," whatever), but my mean parent(s) won't let me." If you don't mind being her parent instead of just her friend, THIS is a WIN – WIN opportunity for you.

The daughter knows, and her friends know, that "Parents" get the last word. They don't have to like it, but they do accept that "Parents" can take decision- making out of their hands. The friends will "blame" the parents and not the daughter for turning them down. They all can pretend how "unjust" her mean parents are, but secretly, the kid that YOU reared may be relieved that you have given her an out. The DAUGHTER is still "accepted," YOU retain authority, and BOTH of you come out of this respected. Your mutual NEEDS to be LOVED and ACCEPTED will be satisfied.

> The daughter knows, and her friends know, that "Parents" get the last word.

> ...look past the negative behaviors of others, to recognize the missing NEED others are trying to meet...

AN ASIDE: Some say it takes a village to raise a child. At the very least it is a partnership between you and the child. YOU provided the boundaries (and the consequences)— your CHILD supplied the behaviors— and the CHILD earned the established consequence (reward/ punishment) YOU promised. When the line between parent and friend gets a little fuzzy, just keep reminding yourself:

"I am the parent... I am the parent... I am the parent..." Later in life, when people tell you how fortunate you are to have such a great kid, remind them that FORTUNE had nothing to do with it; providing the BOUNDARIES (structure) she (he) DEMANDED was the hardest WORK you've ever done!

Remember, children don't just want structure (boundaries) they DEMAND it. In the absence of boundaries (structure), children will act out until it is provided (much more on this subject in subsequent chapters).

Yes, we all choose endless behaviors in the quest to meet our five basic Human NEEDS. But for those of you who choose to look past the negative behaviors of others, to recognize the missing NEED others are trying to meet, YOU shall be called LEADERS and TEACHERS along this path. For those of you who are successful in helping to meet the NEEDS of others will have discovered the secret to the building of positive relationships:

When you work to meet the Needs of OTHERS, you will find that OTHERS will go out of THEIR way to meet YOUR Needs... and they won't even know why they're doing it... Guaranteed!

Chapter 5

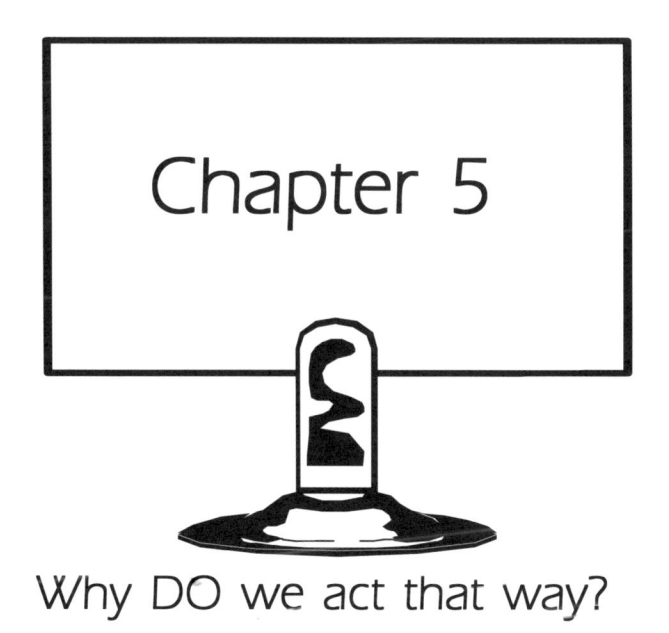

Why DO we act that way?

> *"You can't TALK your way
> out of things that you
> BEHAVED your way into."*
> — Stephen Covey

In a fourteenth century monastery, the Master had been attempting to teach his young student how all of life can be impacted by a single word or a single deed. "THINK," he urged, "before speaking." The student could not imagine how the actions of one person, or one solitary life, could make such a difference. The Master continued, "Once a word or action has been set into motion, it cannot be recaptured. Its impact will go on forever." Still the student could not grasp his meaning.

The patient Master then told his student to take the pillow off his bed, walk it to the tower, and empty the contents from the top window of the tower. Obliging, though confused, the student did as he was asked. At the top of the tower, he took his down-filled pillow, opened the end, and shook its contents into the wind. He then walked back down the stairs to again face his Master.

"As you would cast your words into the wind, have you now cast the feathers into the wind?" asked the Master.

"What did you do THAT for?"

> Once words and action are set into motion, even the most sincere and gracious "I'm sorry," won't bring them back.

"Yes," replied the student, "the wind now carries the feathers."

"Now go," sighed the Master, "return every feather to the pillow."

While it may be possible to recapture every feather, it would be a difficult task, at best. Once words and action are set into motion, even the most sincere and gracious "I'm sorry," won't bring them back.

Over the years I have evaluated schools and school systems on more than a dozen North Central Association of Schools and Colleges (NCA) evaluation teams. Today, the NCA process, including the assembling of "visitation teams," is not even close to the extensive and more laborious methods followed in the "old" days. In the 70's, 80's, and early 90's, NCA evaluations required a team of eight to fifteen educators to descend on a target school for three long school days. In that time, the entire school program was scrutinized.

In different phases of the evaluation process, the panel met with and interviewed teachers, members of the community, parents, and students. It was on one such visit, when the panel was preparing to interview a group of students, that I met Rusty. Before the actual interviews were to begin, one of the members of the evaluation team, in an attempt to put the children at ease, was randomly selecting students and asking friendly, non-threatening questions.

When he got to Rusty, I could see that the boy looked to be about fourteen years old. He was wearing baggy clothes and I couldn't help but notice the several words and drawings etched in ink across his forearms. The knees of his jeans were ripped, his black hair fell in all directions, and his overall slouched posture was sending the message that being unkempt and a non-conformist was cool.

The panel member greeted Rusty, asked how his day had been, how was school, did he like sports, and that sort of thing. After a couple of "It's ok," and "Yeah" replies, Rusty was asked, "Are you doing well in school — are you trying hard?"

A Lesson Plan for understanding what lies behind every behavior.

His answer was firm and matter of fact as he proclaimed, "That's not my STYLE." He then floored me when he continued with, "THEY don't motivate me; THEY can't have me."

Rusty was making it clear that he wasn't about to allow himself to be taught.

I want you to also hear some of what Rusty wasn't saying with his words. In two short sentences Rusty was making a declaration to the world: "If I don't do well in school, if I fail, if I don't proceed to the next grade level, if I don't graduate from high school, marry the girl of my dreams, or end up on in a good paying job, then, well, it's just not MY fault."

To pretend that he didn't care about himself, that he didn't care what others thought about him, was his STYLE. His STYLE was the mask that he wore; the IMAGE he wanted to portray to the world. His IMAGE was his REACTION to how HE felt the world was treating him. He could not fathom that the difference between his STYLE, the image that he wanted to portray—and a productive LIFE-STYLE, a way of life—would be only as far away as his next CHOICE.

Rusty could not accept others as they WERE; he saw them only as he WANTED them to BE. Instead of fitting into the world where the rest of us existed, he wanted the world to revolve around him. Let me repeat that since this is a HUGE factor in the creation of conflict. WE don't accept people as they ARE; we see them only as we WANT them to BE. As long as Rusty CHOOSES to REACT to the world (and there is a little of the resistant Rusty in all of us), rather than RESPOND to the unwelcome behaviors that will ALWAYS come his way, he will forever remain IN conflict.

Inside this angry little boy, there was no vision for tomorrow. He saw tomorrow only as an extension of today. Within his existing pattern of thinking, Rusty could not possibly develop a vision beyond the very moment in which he existed. The decisions he would make tomorrow would be the same decisions he would make today. As long as he remains faithful to his existing pattern of

> "THEY don't motivate me; THEY can't have me."

"What did you do THAT for?"

> Inside this angry little boy, there was no vision for tomorrow. He saw tomorrow as only an extension of today.

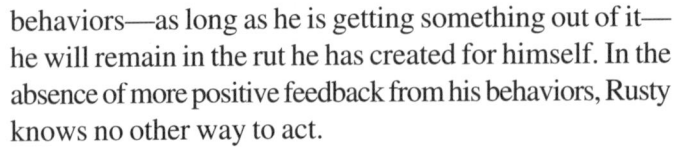

behaviors—as long as he is getting something out of it—he will remain in the rut he has created for himself. In the absence of more positive feedback from his behaviors, Rusty knows no other way to act.

As related in Chapter 3, while it doesn't always happen at a conscious level, we all exercise BEHAVIORS to get our human NEEDS met. To change his current path, Rusty would have to be willing to take a risk — to be willing to try something new — to be willing to risk loss of acceptance, embarrassment, or even loss of status (style). If he believes the risk to be too great, he will remain with behaviors that are already comfortable, even if not always satisfying. Without intervention, or without a reason and the willingness to alter his present cycle of behavior, his future will be little different than his past. CONFLICTS will continue to be viewed as the fault of others.

<u>AN ASIDE</u>: If you have failed at something in the past, it is easy to fall back on that experience and assume that failure would follow you again into your future. In the same manner, when you anticipate failure, knowing what you already HAVE can often be less frightening—even comforting—than knowing that you might fail again. Some would call this a "Self-fulfilling Prophecy."

Fear of rejection and loss of acceptance can polarize us. We adopt the adage, "Better the devil you know than the one you don't know," rather than risk again. That is why some of us readily accept dead-end jobs or repressive relationships. If we have been hurt through past experiences, we might say to ourselves, "Why take a chance on another attempt at seeking happiness when the misery I KNOW can be preferable to the risk I'd be taking?"

Some say Rusty's poor attitude is due to poor upbringing, his parent's fault. Others would say he is the product of a poor environment, peer pressure, television, or those teachers. In fact, they are all right. Rusty is—just like you and me— no more or no less than the sum total of his life's experiences. His repeated experiences reaffirm his attitude, and shape his behaviors. He has CHOSEN a pattern of thinking or a cycle of ineffective behaviors that has formed his attitudes to that moment in his life. Until Rusty recognizes that his behaviors are his CHOICES, NOT his DESTINY, he will remain in a rut, blame others for his failures, and continue to allow his existing behaviors (habits) to shape his future.

Like Rusty, you and I—EVERYDAY—will actually CHOOSE Misery or Happiness. We will choose to either REACT or RESPOND to our experiences (…to the feedback we receive). That is not to say that we don't have very real misery in the world, for there certainly is. But it is not the "event" itself that determines our attitude. We choose the period of sadness we experience from the very real turmoil, disease, sadness, rejection, pain, etc., which affects our lives. It is in our CHOICES to either REACT or RESPOND to the events in our life. *This is what will determine our DECISIONS to choose misery or happiness.* Every day we DECIDE to be the MIRROR for others, or just another REFLECTION of the misery around us.

> Every day we DECIDE to be the MIRROR for others, or just another REFLECTION of the misery around us.

The CYCLE OF HUMAN BEHAVIOR

WHY we choose the BEHAVIORS that we do, as you just read in Chapter 4, is our best attempts to satisfy our inherent drive to meet our basic human NEEDS. The BEHAVIOR CYCLE below illustrates HOW we go about the process of choosing our behaviors.

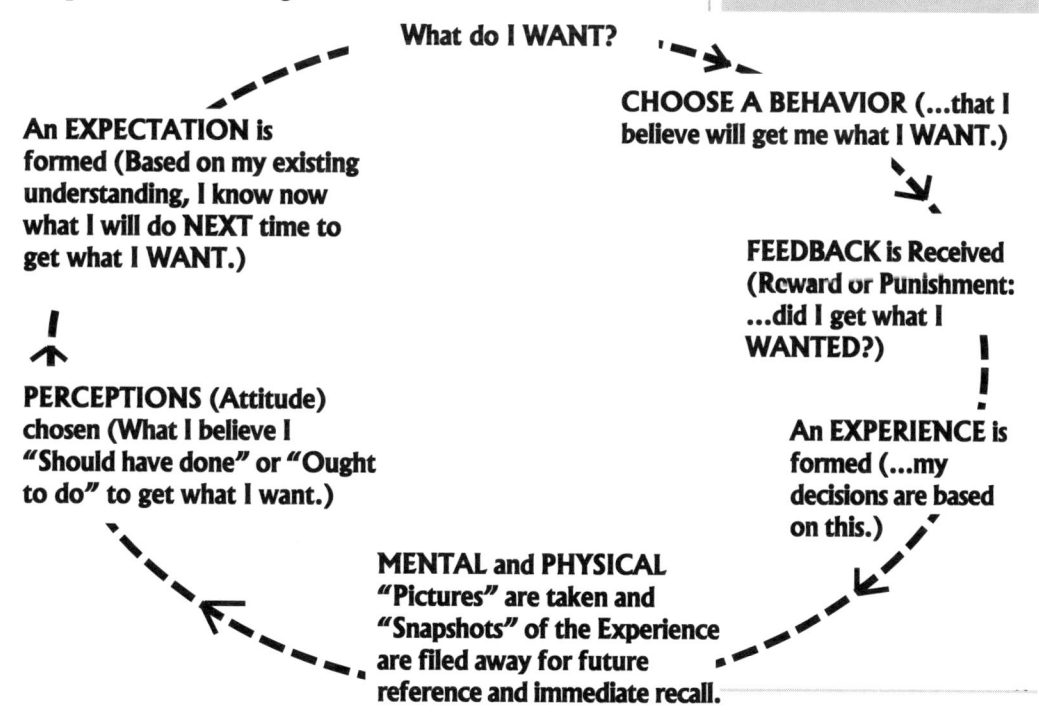

What do I WANT?

CHOOSE A BEHAVIOR (…that I believe will get me what I WANT.)

FEEDBACK is Received (Reward or Punishment: …did I get what I WANTED?)

An EXPERIENCE is formed (…my decisions are based on this.)

MENTAL and PHYSICAL "Pictures" are taken and **"Snapshots"** of the Experience are filed away for future reference and immediate recall.

PERCEPTIONS (Attitude) chosen (What I believe I "Should have done" or "Ought to do" to get what I want.)

An EXPECTATION is formed (Based on my existing understanding, I know now what I will do NEXT time to get what I WANT.)

"What did you do THAT for?"

> ALL behaviors are learned—so ALL behaviors can change.

NOTE: All behaviors are learned ~ so All behaviors can change. The cycle by which we CHOOSE Behaviors, however, will NOT change.

If you'll look at the Behavior Cycle, you will see that you can start anywhere as the Cycle is a loop without end. Since the basic concept, however, calls for an understanding that behaviors start with something we WANT, let's start with something one of our children might want, and later look at what one of our teachers might want. Regardless of age, maturity or experience, the process is the same. Keep one eye on this Behavior Cycle, and follow me through the process. We'll use my son Brian as our example:

➢ **What do YOU WANT?** Make a decision! Let's say that when he was fourteen years old, my son Brian WANTED something he did not have. Since his behaviors are always in pursuit of his NEEDS, let's say he was trying to satisfy his NEED to be Loved and Accepted. I would imagine his thoughts went something like this...
(Brian: I want a...uh, I want...a GIRLFRIEND! Yeah, that's it, I want...a GIRLFRIEND!)

➢ **Choose a BEHAVIOR:** When you decide that you WANT something, if you don't already have it, or if you want more of what you already have, you CHOOSE BEHAVIORS you think will get you what you WANT.
(Brian: To get a GIRLFRIEND, I guess I'd better take a bath and smell better. Then, I'm going into my room and come out lookin' good...even if my bedroom is still a mess. Then I'm going to ask Kerri to go the movies with me.)

A Lesson Plan for understanding what lies behind every behavior.

> **The FEEDBACK you receive**…and there will always be FEEDBACK…will tell you whether or not you now HAVE that which you WANTED (or some of what you wanted).
>
> (Brian: Kerri must have liked the way I smelled and how GOOD I looked, 'cause she said, "YES!")

Connected to the FEEDBACK we receive from our Behaviors is the by-product of decision making known as CONSEQUENCE: Rewards and Punishment. The degree of pleasure or pain we derive from our behaviors is weighed to determine if the BEHAVIOR(S) we chose to get what we WANTED was worth it.

(Brian: So I shocked my family and took some ribbing because I took a bath in the middle of the day and combed my hair for a change. But I was REALLY concerned that Kerri would say "NO." I would have been SOOOO embarrassed [fearing a loss of acceptance]. BUT SHE SAID "YES!")

> **An EXPERIENCE (memory)** of the event is logged and placed in a "database," or the file cabinets of our mind. To the extent we were impacted by the Feedback we received (Rewards vs. Punishment), the EXPERIENCE (memory) will forever remain on our hard drives and ready for recall at a moment's notice.

We place an incredible amount of faith in our Experiences. When change "threatens" us, how many times have you heard people say (or heard YOURSELF say), "But THIS is the way we've ALWAYS done it." Because we have not yet lived to SEE a better or more efficient way, we want to hold on to what our Experience tells us HAS worked or at least is what we already know and are comfortable with (as in the Exodus Story, pg 70).

> …the EXPERIENCE (memory) will forever remain…

> "But THIS is the way we've ALWAYS done it."

(Brian: I wish I hadn't spilled that Pepsi all over her when I tried to put my arm around her… that was dumb! She really wasn't too happy about that. I felt like such a jerk.)

Illustrations by Ashley Teets

➤ **A MENTAL PICTURE i**s taken of the EXPERIENCE as the mind's eye takes a snapshot of the event. This MENTAL PICTURE is "paper clipped" onto the EXPERIENCE we keep "on file." We say a picture is worth a thousand words because it takes at least that many in our attempt to describe the full color PICTURES we saw and felt from the EXPERIENCE.

(Brian: I can STILL "see" that terrible moment when she jumped out of her seat when that cold Pepsi hit her lap. OUCH! How embarrassing. Every time I smell popcorn, it brings the knot back in my stomach—(physical as well as mental pictures of the event). And earlier, when we were standing in that line, she didn't seem too pleased when I started talking to that pretty redhead from our third period class. Wonder why she got so upset? But Kerri told me that I was "cute!")

A Lesson Plan for understanding what lies behind every behavior.

As each of us has different experiences, and different perceptions or frames of reference on life, it is completely understandable how each person involved in the same EXPERIENCE can come away with completely different PICTURES. For example:

> If you think you have been wronged, you will HOLD that "picture" in the picture album you keep in your minds until the wrong has been vindicated.

> If you HOLD a picture of love or acceptance from the past, it will remain in your head until a NEW or BETTER picture (experience) of love and acceptance is permitted to replace the previous picture. It will still be in your album, of course, but in the back of the book, rather than on the cover page of the section of your scrapbook entitled "Love and Acceptance."

> You "carry" the picture of the "Perfect Marriage" with the "Perfect Mate." A man and a woman take two separate "picture albums" of how life was lived to the moment of marriage, then carry those two separate albums of how life "should be" into life with a partner. Is there any wonder where the CONFLICTS in marriage begin? We expect our mate to think and act as WE have learned to think and act. We try to superimpose our OWN pictures over his (or her) pictures and say: our mate "should" pick up his clothes, make spaghetti like mom use to, always put the lid back down...

> If we learned a particular task from someone we admire, we HOLD that picture and say, "If it's good enough for her (him), it's good enough for me."

> You HELD a "picture" of wanting to be a cowboy or a fairy princess until someone or some experience replaced that picture with a newer picture. We tend to "freeze frame" pictures in our heads—hold images...e.g. grudges, loves and sorrows. We often ignore the fact that real life is a non-stop technicolor, full run movie and not a series of black and white snapshots.

> We expect our mate to think and act as WE have learned to think and act.

47

"What did you do THAT for?"

> For EACH of us, it really is... "all about ME."

These pictures or images we carry in our heads are a product of our visual AND physical experiences. Once in our heads, these "pictures" are difficult, if not impossible, to shake. Just as Brian relived the visual picture of the Pepsi dropping in Kerri's lap, he also recalled the emotional embarrassment it generated and the physical knot in his stomach.

AN ASIDE: I think we tend to "see" our memories only as VISUAL pictures and not as a result of our PHYSICAL experiences as well. For example, I remember when I was about 10 years old, I ate WAY too many of those garden fresh green beans I loved so much. Unfortunately, a short time after dinner, it was apparent that I had enjoyed too much of a good thing, and got sick. Although that was 40 years ago, I STILL hold less than positive pictures of green beans. Think back a little bit in your own life. You have PHYSICAL pictures, too, don't you? Physical pain, anguish, torment, aromas, fear, etc., will spark some very powerful memories.

> We develop "an **ATTITUDE:**" As EXPERIENCE is processed through our mental database, the Feedback we received may or may not have been the outcome hoped for from the BEHAVIOR we chose to get us what we WANTED. So, mentally, we back over the game plan to see what went wrong (and right). We evaluate our mistakes and our successes, develop an ATTITUDE and choose our PERCEPTIONS from what we now understand and believe. We say "Eureka! I figured it out—I know what I 'SHOULD HAVE DONE' or 'OUGHT TO DO,' next time, to make it a better experience."

When someone tells you something you find difficult to accept, you become amazed, disappointed, shocked, or whatever, because what you are hearing does not fit the picture of the way (YOU think) it SHOULD BE. Your experiences are based on the perceptions of how life SHOULD BE and on the way people OUGHT to behave in any given situation. This is because—based on what YOU know or understand—this is the way YOU would

A Lesson Plan for understanding what lies behind every behavior.

think, say, or behave. Consequently, you are using yourself as THE standard to judge the actions of all other people. For EACH of us, it really is... "all about ME."

When someone tells you what you SHOULD or OUGHT to do, he (she) is merely telling you what HIS experiences have taught HIM to be the "right" thing to do... in this situation... for HIM. Based on HIS experiences, for what HE knows and understands about the world, this is what HE "Should have done" or "Ought to do." Although this is right for HIM, it may NOT necessarily be "right" for YOU. Internal CONFLICT may arise within YOU if your views differ.

The moment YOU go against your own better judgment and replace YOUR values with the values of those who are telling you what you "SHOULD" do, the seeds of CONFLICT are planted. If their "SHOULDS" are the seeds, YOU are the sower. Only YOU can control YOU. Only YOU can grant permission for the seeds others are sowing to take root in YOU! Why would you allow people to SHOULD all over you?

When your NEED to be accepted by him clashes with what YOUR inner voice is telling you is the "right" thing for YOU to be doing, CONFLICT takes root. That knot in your stomach and the questioning voice within, both are immediate indications that you are IN conflict between what OTHERS (spouse, child, co-worker, parent, boss, etc.) want you to do, and what YOU WANT to do. Whom do you appease? Usually OTHERS—and we comply so willingly!

(Brian: I gotta use a little more class when I do that arm-over-the-seat trick again. I "OUGHT" to put that Pepsi and popcorn on the other side. Maybe I "SHOULDN'T" eat when I'm around her? And she probably just doesn't like redheads (a perception). Yeah, that must be it. I probably "SHOULDN'T" keep telling KERRI just how pretty I think redheads are.)

Whom do you appease?

Usually OTHERS–and we comply so willingly!

"What did you do THAT for?"

> **The BEHAVIOR CYCLE will not change, BUT we CAN change our choices.**

> We form our EXPECTATIONS: We escalate our hopes, become discouraged or hopeful, undeterred and determined, excited or depressed, based on all that has transpired in the formation of this experience. Our Experiences form our Perceptions and Attitudes, and now set our *expectations* for what *we believe* we "should do" next time to get what we *want*.

We allow our past to determine our future each time we say,
   "But this is the way we've always done it!"

>The way I teach school is a reflection of the way MY instructors taught me.
("This is the way I was taught, and it worked for me, so it MUST be the way I should teach—or from those I didn't like—how NOT to teach my students.)

>The way I rear my child is a reflection of the way MY parents reared me. (This would apply even if you practice the opposite lessons you learned from parents. For example, if you thought they were too permissive, you learned from them NOT to be so permissive. If they smoked in the car, you remember how unpleasant that was and told yourself NOT to do the same thing with your kids in the car, etc.)

>Our EXPERIENCES have taught us to EXPECT snow in the winter. We EXPECT to see stars in the sky at night. We EXPECT crowded stores at Christmas, while construction signs tell us to EXPECT Delays. When we get on an airplane, we EXPECT our luggage to arrive when we do (or not!). At a restaurant, we EXPECT good service, while the waiter EXPECTS a tip. We EXPECT our schools to be safe, and EXPECT to live "happily ever after."

(Brian: Next Friday I'll be taking KERRI to the movies again. I just need to remember to use my brother's good-smelling stuff again and comb my hair. Oh yeah, I can't afford another dumb stunt like the Pepsi-in-the-lap trick, and no more talk about redheads!)

Brian's *expectation* for the future, therefore, is based

A Lesson Plan for understanding what lies behind every behavior.

on the *feedback* he received from the *behaviors* he exercised, to get what he *wanted*...a girlfriend. His *experiences* formed his *attitude* as what he "should" do next time. This is the BEHAVIOR CYCLE in action.

> The CYCLE REPEATS: As Brian continues to mature and learn from his Experiences, he will choose to change his behaviors and/or what he WANTS—or he will choose to persist in his existing behaviors. He will ALWAYS have choices.

The BEHAVIOR CYCLE will not change, BUT we CAN change our choices.

Choosing a girlfriend would be a typical fourteen-year-old behavior in an (unconscious) attempt to satisfy a lifelong NEED for Love, Acceptance, and Belonging. It is easy to accept that any fourteen-year-old boy (or girl) would WANT a friend to satisfy this NEED. Many adolescents with limited experiences might make many of the same decisions and draw many of the same conclusions that Brian did in this example. Boy, girl, man, or woman, the same Behavior Cycle demonstrates HOW we process thought.

While the process of thought (the Behavior Cycle) will remain unaltered, the patterns of thought, the actions and habits that are formed from our decisions, most certainly will change. For each time the cycle repeats, it can be altered in three, <u>and ONLY three place</u>s:

In what you WANT…

in the BEHAVIORS you choose…

and/or in what you choose to PERCEIVE (Attitude and Belief).

As we mature and develop and acquire new experiences, our efforts to make more effective and more appropriate behavior choices will follow. As we seek only to satisfy our NEEDS, we will endlessly alter WHAT we think and do.

> As we seek only to satisfy our NEEDS, we will endlessly alter WHAT we think and do.

"What did you do THAT for?"

> It would help if just once in a while I knew that the principal appreciated how hard I work around here.

To demonstrate these three kinds of choices, let's look at how they might be played out through the eyes of a TEACHER.

Let's say that a teacher chooses to WANT something she does not have…or wants more of it. Let's say that she wants to be acknowledged (affirmed, recognized as being important) for all her hard work, dedication, and commitment.

Choice #1: We choose what we WANT?

What do I WANT?
⬇
I CHOOSE A BEHAVIOR
⬇
FEEDBACK is received (Reward or Punishment)
⬇
An EXPERIENCE is formed…
⬇
Create a MENTAL Picture of the Experience
⬇
PERCEPTIONS (Attitude) chosen
⬇
An EXPECTATION formed

The **WANT**: Teacher—All this paperwork, all this pressure on testing and scores, active children, bus duty, hall duty, it's tough to keep up with it all. And I've still got a family of my own to consider! I'm being pulled in so many directions! It's really wearing me out. It would help if just once in a while I knew that the principal appreciated how hard I work around here. <u>What I want (choose) is some respect!</u>"

Choice #2: We choose a BEHAVIOR: "To get the principal's attention, I'm going to prepare a super lesson plan and a really special activity."

What do I WANT?
⬇
I CHOOSE A BEHAVIOR
⬇
FEEDBACK is received (Reward & Punishment)
⬇
An EXPERIENCE is formed...
⬇
Create a MENTAL Picture of the Experience
⬇
PERCEPTIONS (Attitude) chosen
⬇
An EXPECTATION formed

The BEHAVIOR and the FEEDBACK: Teacher— "Well that did a lot of good! The principal didn't come in during the super lesson I taught. Sure, she read the lesson plan, but rather than get noticed, all I got was a big "smiley face" on my plan. BIG DEAL. If that is all the notice I'm going to get, it's just not worth it. "

➢An EXPERIENCE is formed: Teacher— "The kids are great, it's just a shame 'nobody' can see what a great teacher I am."

➢A MENTAL PICTURE of the Experience is formed. Teacher— "The kids performed well. I can see that they are really picking up the concepts I have been working so hard to teach. I'm so proud of them. I really

> The kids are great, it's just a shame "nobody" can see what a great teacher I am.

"What did you do THAT for?"

> That will fix her... and also lift my spirits.

resent, though, that the principal couldn't get off her butt and come to my class to see me in action." (Note: Just because she wanted something, she assumed she would get it.)

Choice #3: We choose "an ATTITUDE."

What do I WANT?
⬇
I CHOOSE A BEHAVIOR
⬇
FEEDBACK is received (Reward & Punishment)
⬇
An EXPERIENCE is formed…
⬇
Create a MENTAL Picture of the Experience
⬇
PERCEPTIONS (Attitude) chosen
⬇
An EXPECTATION formed

The PERCEPTION: Teacher— "The kids would have really enjoyed the principal being in here. I can't wait until my break when I can tell the other teachers just how unconcerned that principal is with the learning that goes on in this building (perception). What does she do all day, anyway?" (Note: Conflict with others can begin just this quickly, and without the person with whom you are in conflict, even being aware of it.)

But wait a minute. In fairness, there are quite a few other teachers in this building she has to work with besides me. And I do know that a school principal's work includes ALL the students, parents, and a ton more paperwork than I have to wade through everyday. Instead of telling other teachers – who can't do a thing about this – I've got another idea. Next time I will be reasonable and personally INVITE her to visit my classroom when I'm doing one of my special lessons. Yeah... great idea!

> We form our EXPECTATIONS... based on our Perception of the situation: Teacher: "If I just tell others, nothing will come from it... except someone might tell her that I was upset and then she would have to come in here and find out why! No, if I really WANT her to come to my room, I will, indeed, INVITE her. Yes, that's what I'll do! I'll tell her she missed a great lesson and ask her to join us NEXT TIME." (Note that in this example the one that talked herself into this conflict also talked herself out of it. In "real life," however, people are not always so quick to see "reason." For once she tells the other teachers how hurt she is, like casting feathers into the wind, even the most sincere, "I'm sorry," won't erase the damage.)

> And the CYCLE REPEATS, each time altering with our CHOICES.

Throughout the countless laps we make around the Behavior Cycle each day, our goal is to meet our NEEDS and grow as human beings. We try not to repeat the errors that we make; instead we try to learn from them. In the same way, we repeat experiences that worked for us. All of this comes out of our persistent drives to satisfy those five (5) basic human NEEDS.

Sooner or later, however, what USED to work for us, won't work anymore. Sooner or later, somebody out there is going to burst our bubble and tell us, "NO."

People often tell us "No," of course, but we so easily brush these aside with simple controlling behaviors that we don't even recognize that it happens. The baby cries, we pick her up; Johnny stomps his foot for ice cream money, you give him a dollar; the wife folds her arms and taps her foot and hubby says, "Yes, dear, is everything all right?" These are all casual, even effortless methods of control, that are so common place that we take both the

> Sooner or later, somebody out there is going to burst our bubble and tell us, "NO."

"What did you do THAT for?"

> For when this day comes, and this day WILL come, like millions of people, you will choose ONE of the following TWO options:

controlling behaviors AND the responses for granted. Though commonplace, they are all, nonetheless, effective methods of controlling others to do what WE want them to do.

So what happens when someone tells you "NO!" and means it?

"NO! You can't have whatever it is you wanted. It is MINE, and I don't want you to have whatever it is YOU think you WANT and SHOULD have. It is NOT yours to take, I'm not giving it to YOU, the answer is NO, and that's final!"

"What's THAT you say?
But I always get what I WANT!
Perhaps you didn't hear me?
I WANT this thing that you won't let me have!"

<u>ENTER CONFLICT:</u> **For when this day comes, and this day WILL come, like millions of people, you will choose ONE of the following TWO options:**

1. You will ACCEPT that you can't have what you want— what someone else possesses and doesn't want you to have— and choose to "WANT" something else.

OR

2. You will ESCALATE and do what many other people choose to do when someone says, "NO, you can't have it!" You will CONTROL to get what you want even though you've already been told "NO, you CAN'T have this thing you want."

A RIDDLE:
"If I can persuade, encourage, manipulate, cajole, or otherwise
CONTROL you to do
what I want you to do...
did I choose your behavior...
or did you?"

Chapter 6

Controlling Behaviors: When you won't take "NO" for an answer.

*Experience is a wonderful teacher.
It enables you to recognize a mistake immediately after you make it again.*

> ...our Behaviors are NOT something that we HAVE to do, but in fact, are our CHOICES...

Before we go any further in describing the METHODS OF CONTROL we ALL use to get what we want, we have to first get past this notion that our behaviors are someone else's responsibility, someone else's fault. We say, "I HAVE to do this, wear that, believe this, or memorize that." Or, "I CAN'T quit my job, earn a higher degree, leave my hometown, or ask Kerri for a date." To really understand this notion that our Behaviors are NOT something that we HAVE to do, but in fact, are our CHOICES, think about this:

Ask yourself, are you going to have a good day on March 19th this year? Not sure? How about on, say, April 18th? Too far away? A dumb question? What if you knew that March 19th was a Monday? If we even mention

> Every behavior is a choice. Some choose happiness—some actually choose to be miserable.

Monday, we act as if our best friend just passed away. If we make a mistake of some kind on this day we say, "What do you expect for a Monday?"

How are you going to feel on April 18th if this is a Friday? It's the middle of the month, maybe a payday, last day of the workweek, WEEKEND... YEAH! All of a sudden, we give over our innate POWER to choose our own happiness to a CALENDAR?

"How are you feeling today?"

"I don't know! Quick, somebody hand me a calendar!"

Every behavior is a choice. Some choose happiness—some actually choose to be miserable.

Imagine you are at home and the phone rings. How many of you will answer that phone because it's ringing? How many of you will answer it because there may be somebody on the other end you want to speak with? Never thought about it? Sure you have. As you start for that phone, you hear a voice inside your head saying, "Oops, wait a minute, that may be my boss, and I'm not supposed to be here." Maybe the voice said, "That may be Aunt Sadie and I need to talk to her." The point is, you THOUGHT about it, and you made a conscious (or subconscious) decision to answer, or NOT to answer.

When my youngest son Brian was fourteen I remember coming home from work to find him on the telephone. In the days before "call waiting" and multiple phone lines, I had been trying to call home for over an hour. When I walked in and saw him on the phone, I realized why I couldn't get through.

"Brian, what's the rule about using the phone?"

"I can't be on the phone more than thirty minutes at a time."

"Right, and you've been on the phone for more than an hour?

"Yeah."

"You know you can't be on the phone more than thirty minutes. This is the third time I told you that you couldn't be on the phone for more than thirty minutes. You are now grounded from the phone. Hang up."

A Lesson Plan for understanding what lies behind every behavior.

"BUT DAD!"

He hesitated a minute, huffed and puffed, we had words, he said a quick good-bye, and slammed the phone down. He then got up, huffed, puffed, and grumbled some more, turned, and STOMPED his feet all the way down the hall, mumbled all the way, disappeared inside his bedroom, and... wait for it... SLAMMED the door! (Any of this sound familiar?)

Now, what was he trying to CONTROL me to do? You've been there; you recognize control when you see it. I didn't CAUSE him to be angry. He could have said, "Oops, sorry, Dad." Instead, he made the conscious choice to try to control. He chose, as this day's method of control, POUTING.

In his adolescent mind, he actually thought that his "woe is me" act was going to compel me to follow him back to his room, throw open the door and plea, "Oh, SON, gracious goodness me, I have sinned against thee! I don't know what came over me. Please forgive the rashness of your father for he has caused great sadness in your life. I don't know how I can live with myself. Please forgive me!" Yeah, RIGHT!

> I no more CAUSED him to be angry and POUT, than I can CAUSE YOU to answer a telephone merely because it's ringing.

In fairness to Brian (remember the Behavior Cycle), he had been on the phone more than thirty minutes twice before. But because he had not been grounded after the first two times, his previous FEEDBACK—twice now—was, "Dad doesn't really mean it." Therefore, his EXPECTATION was that he wouldn't be grounded THIS time either. On this third occasion he was grounded, leaving him with those two choices: He could *respond* or *react*. He could decide to either *respond* by ACCEPTING the consequences of his actions, or *react* by trying to CONTROL me to reconsider. Relying on past experience, he chose CONTROL.

While I didn't CAUSE Brian to become angry, I DID confuse him by sending mixed messages. He knew

"What did you do THAT for?"

> It is amazing how much smarter we parents become AFTER our children are grown.

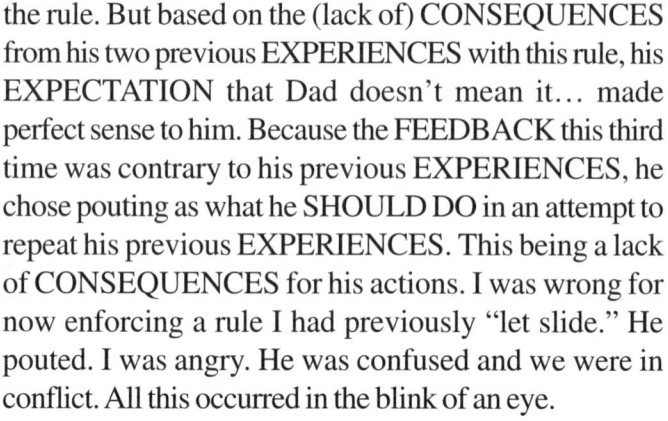

the rule. But based on the (lack of) CONSEQUENCES from his two previous EXPERIENCES with this rule, his EXPECTATION that Dad doesn't mean it… made perfect sense to him. Because the FEEDBACK this third time was contrary to his previous EXPERIENCES, he chose pouting as what he SHOULD DO in an attempt to repeat his previous EXPERIENCES. This being a lack of CONSEQUENCES for his actions. I was wrong for now enforcing a rule I had previously "let slide." He pouted. I was angry. He was confused and we were in conflict. All this occurred in the blink of an eye.

If my wife and I had really understood how important this parenting stuff was at the time of his birth, we would have paid more attention to the "Parenting Manual" that came home from the hospital with him. (I made that manual thing up… don't go looking for it…) But had we allowed him to accept the natural consequences of his actions the FIRST time, Brian would not have been so confused by the "grounding."

If, for example, Brian had a history of being TAUGHT that the natural consequence of being on the phone for more than thirty minutes would be "grounding from the phone," his behavior for being "busted" would have been far more appropriate. The natural consequence for his behavior, as all behavior is learned, would have been his EXPECTATION. He would have been far more likely to ACCEPT, rather than attempt CONTROL. (And that could have been the end of it, eliminating the need to later mend the interpersonal conflict that I had to accept some responsibility for creating.)

It is amazing how much smarter we parents become AFTER our children are grown.

AN ASIDE: There are just a few absolutes in life. One of them is this: Although they won't admit it, kids (all of us really) don't just want STRUCTURE or BOUNDARIES in their lives — they demand it. If they don't get it, they will REACT by acting out until they get it... Guaranteed!

A Lesson Plan for understanding what lies behind every behavior.

If you are a teacher, ever notice in your schools how the same child might act out in one classroom, yet not in another? When that child exhibits acting out behaviors in your classroom, I assure you, the behaviors of that one child...which can quickly become contagious and spread to others...are a CLEAR message to you. He (she) is demanding that you RESPOND to his actions by providing STRUCTURE. YOU provide the structure... the limits or BOUNDARIES of your classroom, and then allow the child the freedom to choose his/her own behaviors within those boundaries.

While you may not be able to completely provide STRUCTURE (boundaries) in his life, you CAN RESPOND to his behaviors by providing what he needs now: limits in this, his classroom. He needs it and is counting on YOU to provide the BOUNDARIES (structure). He will, in fact, continue to REACT with these acting out, disruptive, and controlling behaviors until you do RESPOND to what *he* doesn't even realize he is acting out for: STRUCTURE.

If you teach (not just tell) a child "NO, you can't have this thing you want...." YOU have just taught the child a BOUNDARY. Expect, then, the Boundary to be pushed...for the limits to be tested. "Please, I really want this thing you won't let me have!" If you next say, "Oh, ok, I give up, you can now have this thing you want that I said you could not have," what did you really *teach* the child? You have taught the child that "No" means "Yes." The child has further taught YOU that to get his/her boundaries moved, all he/she has to do is to keep pushing. Because if YOU are not firm or sure of the boundaries, how could you expect the child to know what they are?

> ...then allow children the freedom to choose their own behaviors within those boundaries.

ARE YOU STAYING HOME FROM SCHOOL?
YEAH I'M SICK.

SICK OF TOO MUCH PIZZA, SODA, AND ICE CREAM? I TOLD YOU...

WHY IS IT SOME PEOPLE AREN'T HAPPY UNTIL THEY CAN POINT OUT YOUR MISERY.

"What did you do THAT for?"

> ...fail to provide the promised, earned, and anticipated consequences, then YOU...not your child(ren)...moved the BOUNDARIES.

"The Parent/Teacher's Guide"

**YOU establish the BOUNDARIES
with your children.
(Home or Classroom Rules)**

**YOU TEACH the BOUNDARIES
to your children.
(Consequences: Rewards and Penalties)**

**CHILDREN will CHOOSE their own
BEHAVIORS.**

**CHILDREN must receive the promised,
earned, and anticipated consequences for
those behaviors
(Rewards and Penalties).**

**If YOU fail to provide the promised, earned,
and anticipated consequences, then
YOU...not your child(ren)...moved the
BOUNDARIES.**

You DO know where CONTROL comes from, don't you?

I think CONTROL began with one mother and child. They travel around the country visiting different stores and outlets; you're bound to have seen them. You may have seen them in the checkout line in your local grocery store.

The little one, sitting so demurely in the seat of the grocery cart, eyes the candy while Mommy waits patiently for her turn to pay for her groceries. The child points to a candy bar and says, "Mommy, I want one."

Mother, the adult in charge, says, "No, you can't have one."

Now, keep your eye on the child. You will literally (almost), SEE the Behavior Cycle working inside her little body: The little one pulled up a previous memory from her *Experience* or "memory database," processed the *Feedback* she just received from Mom (...and there will

A Lesson Plan for understanding what lies behind every behavior.

always be Feedback), and recalled another occasion when she ate candy and enjoyed it. She also SAW herself in a previous situation when she told Mom that she "wanted" something and mom said "No." In a flash, she weighed the *Feedback* (rewards vs. punishment), and in doing so, formed a new Expectation. She knew what she *Wanted*, refused to accept NO for an answer, chose a new Behavior (CONTROL), and plunged forward in raised voice.

"Mother, I WANT one!"

Mother, feigning agitation, says, "NO, you can't have one."

Now the wheels really begin to turn in that little one. Keep watching her process the past experiences and this brief exchange. (Remember, she has only two choices: She can ACCEPT "NO" and change what she WANTS, or she can choose CONTROL in an attempt to get what she wants, even though Mom already told her "NO, you can't have it.") Just keep watching this little girl and you will instantly realize that she's not finished yet. Choosing to persist (to control), she stomps her foot and for a third time cries, "MOTHER, I WANT ONE!"

As onlookers develop an increased interest in the exchange (Gee, do you think the child LEARNS to take advantage of that… hmmm), Mother hopes still to appear in control of the situation. Mother is now about to make one of the biggest decisions of her life, and she doesn't even know it. She contradicts herself and says, "Oh, OK, but you can only have ONE."

If you're not in too big of a hurry, just stick around a minute longer and watch the child file that experience into her "database." What do you think she will do next? RIGHT! There is a good chance that the very next words out of her mouth will be, "MOTHER, I WANT TWO!"

Mother rationalizes that she is still in charge and can end this public debate by getting in the last word. (We humans believe that if we get in the LAST word… or the LOUDEST word… that we will win a debate.) One more time she confuses the child and exclaims, "OK, but you can only eat them in the car!"

> Mother is now about to make one of the biggest decisions of her life...

"What did you do THAT for?"

> Remember, in the absence of clear boundaries, (structure), a child WILL act out until structure is provided.

Now... What did Mother just TEACH her child?

That "NO" means "YES" if you ask three times and stomp your foot once!

Now I know you've seen this mom and her child at least once in your local grocery store. I know you have because you were overheard to have said, "If that were MY child I'd..."

Perhaps you saw her a little later in life, when the child was a bit older. That would be the child that has, by this time, LEARNED to escalate CONTROL by lying down in the middle of the aisle, thrashing her arms and legs and wailing because mother won't buy something else she wants...and HAS to have... RIGHT NOW! Remember, in the absence of clear boundaries, (structure), a child WILL act out until structure is provided.

Let me insert here that many people might define CONTROLLING BEHAVIORS as negative and manipulative means to a selfish end. Actually, we probably use CONTROL more commonly to meet the positive wants in our lives. When the child on the playground falls to the ground — BEFORE he cries — what does he do? He looks up at YOU, to see if YOU are worried or frightened. He is looking to see if YOU will panic or smile. You're clapping, and making wisecracks to encourage a grin from the one who has just toppled off the sliding board is an attempt to divert (control) a frown into a smile. He is "waiting" for YOU to tell him whether or not he is hurt. YOUR actions serve to control HIS actions.

You'll recognize CONTROL in so many other ways as well. You whistle for the dog in hopes he will come wagging his tail. You wave at the neighbor anticipating a wave in return. When a small child is sad, she will offer the cutest little puckering of her lower lip that screams for a hug. When you greet students in the morning with a warm smile and friendly greeting, you fully expect to be rewarded with the same positive behaviors in return. When Emily, our grandchild, wants her grandmother to read a book to her, she reaches for a book and her blanket and steps over to the rocking chair. This is the perfect cue for

A Lesson Plan for understanding what lies behind every behavior.

"controlling" her Grammy into curling up with her for a story.

In Asia, in order to capture a monkey, you build a small cage and stake it to the ground. You then put a banana in the cage and wait. Soon, a monkey will come by, squeeze his hand between the bars, and grab the banana. To avoid capture and ultimately being boiled for dinner, the monkey has only to release his grip, pull his hand back, and run away. His stubborn refusal to release CONTROL of the fruit is what will lead to his capture...and to his death.

As individuals, if we want what we cannot have, we figure ways to control people so they will give us what they didn't want us to have. It is perfectly natural...up to a point. Psychologists have a word for it, however, when it becomes a fixation—like a monkey that would rather die than release control of what is within his grasp. When we humans won't let go, it is called LOSS of INSIGHT.

The "Levels" below demonstrate the stages of Conflict we travel through when we persist in our attempts to CONTROL. Understand that each time we take a step to the next level of CONTROL, we are using an endless array of CONTROLLING METHODS (behaviors) that we believe will work for us, to convince others to give us what they already told us we can't have. THINK ABOUT IT. What works for you? Crying, pouting, manipulation, threats, rejection, pleading, silence, anger, screaming, seduction, intimidation, guilt?

AN ASIDE: Guilt is a popular method of Control. Remember the definition of Guilt: GUILT is when OTHERS are trying to make YOU responsible for THEIR Needs. Guilt happens to be one of my favorites: "Son, will you wash my car for me? If you can't, that's all right. I'll probably hurt my back again with all the bending over I'll have to do, but don't worry, please, I haven't been laid up for weeks. NO, really, you just sit your young self down there. I'm sure there is only a small risk of pneumonia with that cold water and this chilly air at my age so please, don't worry, I'll probably not die."

CONFLICT begins when someone tells us "NO" and he/she won't take "NO" for an answer.

"What did you do THAT for?"

When someone tells you "NO"– You can RESPOND by...

CONFLICT begins when someone tells us "NO" and he/she won't take "NO" for an answer. We all do it to some degree, of course, and can do so without risking CONFLICT with self or others. (How do you think Tom Sawyer got those other kids to whitewash that fence for him?)

Most administrators, for example, know that to avoid conflicts, they must at times release CONTROL (of decisions, programs, and committees), in order to maintain AUTHORITY.

Remember, you will ALWAYS have CHOICES

When someone tells you "NO"...
You will choose to either
ACCEPT "No" for an answer,
or you will ESCALATE
in further attempts to
control.

The Stages of the Escalation of Control

Level 1: When someone tells you "NO" —You can RESPOND by…

Accepting "NO" for an answer, even if you don't agree, or change behaviors to want something else,

OR

You will escalate and REACT by…
Choosing a behavior intended to CONTROL to get what you want. i.e., crying, pouting, guilting, stomping your feet, slamming doors, etc.

Level 2: If someone still says "NO"–You can RESPOND by…

Accepting "NO" for an answer, even if you don't agree, or change behaviors to want something else,

A Lesson Plan for understanding what lies behind every behavior.

OR

You will REACT by... escalating your method of CONTROL.

This raises the stakes by increasing the level of pressure (Control) exerted to acquire whatever it is you want, but he/she won't let you have. It also increases the pressure on the relationship between you and the person who won't let you have this thing you want.

> If reasoning fails to tell you that you can't CONTROL this human being, you will REACT by...

Level 3: If your previous efforts to persist have failed and someone still tells you "NO," you can then RESPOND by...

Accepting (finally) "NO" for an answer, even if you don't agree, or change behaviors to want something else,

OR

You will REACT by... escalating your method of CONTROL. The attempts to Control rise to subtle manipulation, non-verbal suggestions, and veiled implications. You are now approaching "Loss of Insight."

Level 4: If your previous efforts to persist have failed and someone still tells you "NO," you can then RESPOND by...

Accepting (finally) "NO" for an answer, even if you don't agree, or change behaviors to want something else,

OR

If reasoning still fails to tell you that you can't CONTROL this human being, you will REACT by... further escalating methods of CONTROL.

Internal Conflict released, open hostility, relationships jeopardized, name calling, intimidation, displays of anger, threats and verbal attacks are all evident.

"What did you do THAT for?"

YOU can ALWAYS be in control of YOU!

Level 5: If you choose to persist in your Controlling Behaviors, still refusing to accept another human being's right to deny to you what he/she has...and chooses to keep...there is little hope at this level you will RESPOND by finally accepting "NO" for an answer, and change behaviors to want something else.

Therefore,

As PRIDE forbids you from backing down, and REASON fails to tell you that PRIDE is also what is inhibiting him/her from giving in to YOUR pressure, you will again REACT by...

Further escalating CONTROL.

Final Level: Open hositility, character assasination, alienation, sides formed with co-workers, family and community, walls are built, and a visible shift occurs from Conflict to Violence.

YOU can ALWAYS be in control of YOU!

"You will either ACCEPT...even if you don't agree...or you will choose to ESCALATE."

A Lesson Plan for understanding what lies behind every behavior.

Chapter 7

So, what do YOU Want ?

"The purpose of education is to open people to an acceptance that they CAN achieve whatever they UNDERSTAND and BELIEVE."

I recently participated in a tri-state education staff development conference held in a large convention center in downtown Columbus, Ohio. In between my workshop sessions I glanced through the conference program of events and presentations and was struck by the title of a workshop being conducted for school secretaries. The session was entitled, "Is your life out of balance? Take the flat tire survey." The title caught my attention, I was curious, that session was about ready to start, I had plenty of time before my next session, so I went looking for a room full of secretaries. I finally found that room number and slid into the last open seat in the back row. As I looked around, I was only one of very few males in the room. With some of the glances I got, I was beginning to think this wasn't such a good idea after all. I felt like a kid without a hall pass as the session had already begun.

"What did you do THAT for?"

> It is all about choosing to repeat habits that she is comfortable with, rather than choosing to seek new behaviors to break away from the past.

The chalk board in the front of the room said, in essence, that this session dealt with the need to find "balance in life between work, home and leisure." (Putting that in terms of our basic human NEEDS, this would be a balance between our NEED for Love and Acceptance, our NEED to be Fulfillment and Affirmed, and the NEED for Fun in our lives.) I got there in time to hear one of my fellow students, Judy, make the following declaration:

"About three years ago, after realizing that I was dedicating too much time to my work, I cut back my workday to a half day. I wanted to have more time to make dinner for my family every night, help my kids with homework, and spend more time with my husband. Three years later, I returned again to working full time. After a while, dinner returned to being cooked only twice a week, the table was still stacked with unfinished paperwork, and my husband and I referred to us as 'ships passing in the night.' Why is that?"

The presenter responded to Judy by addressing the group. She told everyone that "Out of habit, Judy was returning to what was comfortable for her." And that she "must be getting something out of it (her existing behaviors), or she wouldn't keep repeating them." Very good response, I thought. It is all about choosing to repeat habits that she is comfortable with, rather than choosing to seek new behaviors to break away from the past. We remain in repressive relationships and unsatisfactory stations in our life because we choose to stay with what is comfortable.

The session was very good, but I remember thinking that the participants did not go home with an understanding as to HOW they could 'break away' from old habits and build new ones.

Do you remember the Exodus story from the Bible? Moses led his people out of slavery, across the Sea, and out into the wilderness. Year after year, the people wandered and became more and more discouraged because the Promised Land wasn't around the next bend. Discouraged, they wanted to return to Egypt and slavery. It wasn't that they liked slavery; in fact, they jumped at

A Lesson Plan for understanding what lies behind every behavior.

the chance to leave it behind. But in moments of uncertainty, wandering about aimlessly as people without direction, they had to wonder, "Was it worth it?" (remember the Behavior Cycle...)

WANTED: freedom from slavery...

FEEDBACK: got freedom...

CONSEQUENCES: was it worth it???

They didn't like slavery, but in moments of despair, many wanted to return to Egypt. They wanted to return to what they KNEW... to what they *understood*. And what they understood was preferably to the unknown that lay ahead.

Without knowing where they were going, without a map to make it there, they fell back to what was comfortable for them. Currently experiencing despair, and having never actually experienced a "Promised Land" before, they were willing to return to what they DID know —what they had *already* experienced—rather than holding on to the goal and what they COULD have. (EXPERIENCE: holds that metal picture of the way it "used to be"...)

Judy was surprised that just because she "decided" that a life-style change was *needed*, it didn't just happen. Without a plan, however, the initial excitement of something hoped for was overshadowed by the tough reality of the day-to-day grind through the wilderness to get to *her* Promised Land. Judy wanted to know *why* she had fallen into the same routine again, why she had returned to the same slavery or drudgery that only a short while ago she was so enthused about leaving. Could it be because the flash-in-the-pan idea to do these wonderful things for herself and her family was just that, a noble gesture and a wonderful *idea*—NOT a GOAL she was willing to commit to? As Mark Twain might have said it, "Maybe she just don't want it bad enough."

> Judy was surprised that just because she "decided" that a life-style change was *needed*, it didn't just happen.

"What did you do THAT for?"

> If she truly wants a change, the answer to this next question has to be "Yes."

If Judy were to read this now, I would ask her to answer these questions:

1. Judy, **WHAT DO YOU WANT?**

Presuming her answer is still what she intended above (less work, more time with family), the next question is…

2. **WHAT ARE YOU DOING ABOUT IT?**

Judy's NEEDS (…her NEEDS being different from her BEHAVIORS), may be the *love and acceptance* of her family, to rediscover some *fun* in her life, or to find some of the *freedom* in her life that a ten-hour work day wasn't permitting. What she was doing was to cut down to a half day and declare a desire to spend more time at home.

3. This is the biggy: **IS WHAT YOU ARE CURRENTLY DOING, WORKING FOR YOU?**

Judy cut back her workday and was off to a great start. So what happened? Why isn't it working now? What's missing? Her answer then, is "NO," it's not working. Her needs are still not being met.

4. If she truly wants a change, the answer to this next question has to be "Yes:" **ARE YOU READY TO MAKE A *PLAN*?** (A PLAN that *will* meet her needs.)

Judy had high hopes, knew what she wanted, and was willing to work hard to get it. But without a map to get there, it would be no different than being lost in downtown Columbus. She could have high hopes, she could drive really fast, she could work at it for long hours, but without a map—a way to determine whether or not she was making progress—she would STILL be *LOST*.

As Judy begins to accept that she is lost, her mood will change, her hopes will fade, and her anxiety will mount. "How easy it would be," she thinks, "to simply turn around

A Lesson Plan for understanding what lies behind every behavior.

and go home, a place I know, where I am comfortable and my surroundings are familiar to me." Without experience to guide her or a map marking her destination, she will know neither where she is going nor the progress she is making. She can only HOPE she will make it. Destinations reached without a map are arrived at only by CHANCE.

When we humans choose to repeat similar behaviors over long periods of time, we form routines: predictable habits. These habits become our conditioned responses rather than conscious behaviors. We will repeat what is "comfortable" as long as we continue to "get *something* out of it." People resist change because they do not know if what CAN BE gained will be better than what they already have. The risk that we might FAIL in our attempt to achieve something better can be as frightening as losing whatever it is we now hold. It is the age-old question: am I content with "the bird in the hand," or should I risk it for "the two in the bush?" Judy might know what she WANTS, but she must first decide how motivated she is to EARN it. In a manner of speaking, without realizing it, either way, she is planning. She will either PLAN to succeed, or, in the absence of a plan...she can *PLAN on* falling back into her old habits again.

Think of it as digging a ditch, one shovel full at a time. Habits take a long time to form...Weeks? Months? Years? Without a concerted effort to break unproductive habits, and a PLAN as to how that will happen (and keep that happening daily), Judy won't be able to fill in that ditch and start over merely because she *decided* to.

If it were that easy, how many people who said they were going to be starting that diet today... *actually did?* If you started last week, are you still on it? If not, it may be because you have to do more than DECIDE to do it. It takes a plan, a conscious effort and hard work, every day, until THAT new habit (and it takes twenty-one days to build that new habit), is formed.

Once she DECIDES to commit to what she WANTS, Judy must next make a PLAN, a road map, as to what she will do to get what she wants. She must then be committed to following that plan (goal)...*until she gets*

>...it takes twenty-one days to build that new habit...

"What did you do THAT for?"

> ... when you become firmly rooted in your new habits, you will be AMAZED at the JOY and inner PEACE you will not only be bringing to yourself, but to your family as well!

there. With her family, she must start with a *DAILY* plan that will take her step by step—one day at a time—to her overall goal (plan) of staying home, feeding her family, and having more time with her husband and kids. If a detour comes up along the way to your goal, make those adjustments with confidence, as the detour ultimately is designed to return you back to the main road. Your destinations (goals) remain the focus... not the detours.

As she follows her daily plan, consistent *habits*, not just *hopes*, are built. Each DAY she gets stronger, more confident, with successful experiences behind her and positive expectations in front of her. When she is comfortable with this terrain, she will be ready to expand her map and prepare *bi-weekly* plans— then *weekly* goals—— until the habits she is NOW choosing become the *lifestyle* she has always wanted.

Keep the map in hand, Judy. If this is what you REALLY want, *no one* can keep you from it, but YOU. I encourage you to become VERY familiar with the map you've developed and the direction in which you're headed. Periodically, it is OK to ask yourself those four questions again to confirm your direction or to make those small detours that will return you to the path you want. Just keep in mind, if you are committed to making it all the way to your destination, but ignore your plan, this will only be another well-intended attempt.

I promise you Judy, when you become firmly rooted in your new habits, you will be AMAZED at the JOY and inner PEACE you will not only be bringing to yourself, but to your family as well! That alone, may be sufficient motivation to continue.

So, what do YOU want?
Are YOU ready to make a change?

Many of us have chosen NOT to set goals (make a plan) for ourselves. Goal setting serves to show us the destination — or a series of destinations — we hope to reach in our lifetime. It's not that we don't WANT to, it's just easier NOT to. Instead, we just plod along each day, almost instinctively following a ROUTINE rather that a

A Lesson Plan for understanding what lies behind every behavior.

ROUTE. We arise in the morning and simply chase our daily obligations that lead us in circles instead of a path that will take us closer to realizing our dreams. Either way, *both avenues are choices*… and EACH of us has the *freedom* (NEED) to choose his or her own road.

Are you ready now to take CHARGE of YOU?

If YOU are ready to put yourself back in control of your *own* life, you ARE "ready to take charge of YOU." To do that, you must *start* by sitting down, taking a few minutes (and a deep breath), and drawing yourself a MAP (a PLAN).

Are you ready now to make a PLAN?

The MAP you are about to make will remain your guide, revealing in black and white for all to see, exactly where YOU want to go, and how YOU intend to get there. With a *MAP*, you have a *PLAN*. Without a PLAN how could you possibly know where you are… or where you're going?

What follows is a simple, STEP by STEP approach to "drawing" your own MAP.

FIRST, for EACH goal you have, ask yourself: **"What do I WANT?"**

Take your time and *really* think it through. Then begin mapping it out—*literally writing it out*—HOW you intend to get there. There are only four simple questions to answer (from page 72), so give it a try. (Remember, answer all four questions for EACH goal.)

Are you ready now to make a PLAN?

> As you become ...in charge of the direction your life is headed, ...you will become more comfortable in your choices for the life you have chosen...

1. WHAT do I *really* WANT?

2. WHAT am I currently DOING about getting this thing I WANT?

3. Is what I'm doing now, working for me to get this thing I WANT?

4. No? Then I'll make a PLAN (step by step) to get this thing I want?
(Literally, write it out, **Step by Step,** what you intend to do to reach this Goal... this thing you *really* want.
Note: If it takes more than 3-5 Steps, then your Goal (your WANT) is too broad.)

a.

b.

c.

d.

e.

If you have been "LOST" for some time, you may have to refer to this MAP every day for a while. You can make appropriate course changes along the way, but the GOAL... that which you said you *really* wanted... remains the focus. Adjust your plan when necessary by acknowledging when steps are completed, and when difficult steps need more of your attention. If you focus your attention on completing EACH step, you will not only reach your goal, there is no way you cannot!

As you become more accustomed to the idea of being in charge of the direction your life is headed, of *being behind the wheel and in charge of which way to turn,* the *controls* of your car will become more comfortable in your grip. When the road you now travel becomes more familiar, your day-to-day reliance on the MAP will taper to a couple of days a week, or once a month, or only occasionally.

Keep your MAP posted for daily reference.

Post it on the refrigerator, on your bedroom or bathroom mirror, on your desk or counter top in a special "MAP" holder. But keep your MAP (GOALS) in front of you at all times! Don't apologize for it because this really is...

ALL About YOU! And that's OK, because *EVERYONE* will benefit!

**If you follow your map,
you WILL achieve your goal
(and get more of what you NEED
along the way).**

Human Resource Leadership Consultants

Business and education Staff Development seminars *guaranteed* to improve *UNDERSTANDING* among and between people. This popular, fast paced, and fun *"The Teacher Down the Hall"* seminar series has been presented to thousands of school and business employees across the country and has been specifically designed to build better *relationships, productivity, and teamwork*.

1. "What did you do THAT for?"

Recognize the difference between our human NEEDS and our human BEHAVIORS. You can't be expected to understand every human behavior...but you CAN easily understand these five basic Needs. Be willing to look behind the negative or inappropriate behaviors of others, to help OTHERS meet THEIR Needs, and *THEY* will go out of their way to meet *YOUR* Needs...*Guaranteed!*

2. "So THAT'S why you're like that!"

This includes true stories of interpersonal conflict and the resolution of conflict, offering incites into Understanding, Accepting, and Resolving CONFLICT.

3. "Excuse me? Did you just say what I thought I saw?"

Personal and professional relationships are dependent upon understanding OTHERS and how OTHERS are to understand us. A thousand times a day we speak through our Words, Inflection, and Body Language (non-verbals). Hear what others are really saying to you...even when they're saying nothing at all.

4. *LISTEN*...and become the TALK of the town.

True communications and understanding is *never* in the intent of the speaker; it is *always* in the message received by the listener. We humans NEED to *relate* to each other. Relationship will be built and conflicts resolved when you practice these four "A's" of Active Listening. You will be amazed how *OTHERS* will begin treating *YOU* differently, more positively, and *THEY* won't even know why they're doing it...*Guaranteed!*

Work Shop Series

5. Personality Profiles: "Can't we all just get along?"

Our human BEHAVIORS are what keep us apart; our human NEEDS are what we have in common. But it is our PERSONALITIES that give us balance. In this active, fun and highly charged hands-on seminar, participants will learn their own personality traits, and the traits of those around them. Participants will immediately discover why some people excel in certain tasks, yet flounder in others. And the question will be answered as to why you choose to admire and respect some folks...yet remain in conflict with others.

- ☞ All seminars are fun, fast paced, and guaranteed to be "user friendly."

- ☞ Tod Faller has been conducting Communication, Leadership, and Motivation programs and seminars for business, schools and school systems since 1986.

- ☞ He has already presented in more than 40 of West Virginia's 55 school systems.

To arrange a workshop/seminar contact:

Human Resource Leadership Consultants
3005 Brierwood Rd., Culloden, WV 25510
www.todfaller.com
Email: tod@todfaller.com

HRL Human Resource Leadership Consultants

PRESENTS

Seminars, Workshops,
Keynote presentations providing
Motivation*Leadership*Communication

Books:

It's ALL About YOU!
"What did you do THAT for?"
"So THAT'S why you're like that!"—Publication date 2005

TOD FALLER has been a national presenter, providing Communication, Leadership, and Motivation seminars, from Green Bay to Jacksonville, since 1986. His Seminar Series provides conflict resolution solutions through an understanding and acceptance of the nature of our Human Behavior.

All seminars are fast paced, "user friendly," and GUARANTEED!

If you would like to be added to the mailing list for future publications, video tapes, and CDs by Tod Faller, please send us an email to *maillist@headlinebooks.com* with the subject line, "Add me to your list."

If you have questions, would like further information, or would like Tod to speak with your school, business or organization, please contact us at:

Human Resource Leadership Consultants
3005 Brierwood Rd., Culloden, WV 25510
www.todfaller.com
Email: tod@todfaller.com

Headline Books, Inc.

P. O. Box 52
Terra Alta, WV 26764
800-570-5951 www.headlinebooks.com